GO AHEAD...
PICK ME UP!

PUT ME IN YOUR BACKPACK!

Inspiring Ways to

Pick Yourself Up and Feel Your Best

Praise for GO AHEAD…PICK ME UP!
PUT ME IN YOUR BACKPACK!

"Reading this book was like talking to a friend … Whatever phase of life you are in, this book will give you solid, relatable tools to use to deal with issues and enrich your life."
–Helaine T, Amazon customer

"An inspiring self-help book designed for individuals seeking to enhance their well-being and fulfilment."
–Swapna Peri, Book Reviews Cafe on Goodreads

"The writing style was positive and encouraging. I enjoyed reading the book and thought it was informative and uplifting." **–Lola's Reviews**

"What a delightful read for any age or any stage of life. So many people relate better to music than just words … I would highly recommend this gem to everyone I know."
–JoJo, Amazon customer

"It is the kind of book you can dip in and out of. I think it will offer something for everyone. Enjoyable, inspiring and worthwhile." **–Rona, reviewer on Goodreads**

"Dr. Boehm writes with a warmth and sincerity that makes her advice feel personal and relatable. This book is perfect for readers of all ages and layered with practical, actionable information." **–Jessyca B, Amazon customer**

"This book will inspire anyone on the journey called life. It is full of tips, strategies, and exercises that will help us to navigate life and all it has to offer … A good read and I highly recommend." **–Native Texan, Amazon customer**

GO AHEAD...
PICK ME UP!

PUT ME IN YOUR BACKPACK!

Inspiring Ways to

Pick Yourself Up and Feel Your Best

Dr. Pamela J. Boehm

Publisher's Note

This publication is designed to provide information in regard to the subject matter covered. It is sold with the understanding that the publisher is not engaged in rendering professional counseling services. If counseling services are needed, it is recommended services should be sought by a professional.

Names have been changed to various degrees in order to protect the confidentiality of the individuals who inspired the stories in the book.

Dedication

*"People don't care how much you know
until they know how much you care."*

—Theodore Roosevelt

I would like to express my appreciation to all those who have helped me with my first manuscript. My gratitude to Hill College for a wonderful 41 years of employment and to be able to tell stories of the many students that I came in contact with over those years.

I am also deeply appreciative for the exceptional contributions of my consultant Brian Moreland, who gave exceptional advice and believed I could get this accomplished.

My deepest gratitude to my editor, Melanie Saxton, whose interest in this book arises from a genuine dedication to helping me, who was a perfect fit for this type of book.

Finally, a special thank you to my mom, family and friends, whom are my rock and support in all of my undertakings. You know who you are.

Contents

Introduction

This book is for **YOU!** That's right, **YOU!** Any of **YOU!** Anyone who ever felt they were not good enough. Anyone who felt they didn't measure up. Anyone who wondered if they would ever amount to anything. Anyone who might need a pick me up!

Take it from me, a counselor, teacher, and former administrator. This "pick-me-up" notion is the foundation of everything on the pages below, along with themes of music and "tools" for thriving.

Have you ever thought about how many things you pick up in a day? You picked up your coffee this morning and you picked up your wallet, a pen, and a receipt. Or you picked up your cell phone and checked messages and texts, etc.

There was a reason you picked up this book as well. You were looking for something. Perhaps you like to read, and the title caught your eye. Maybe you're not feeling fulfilled and are wondering why any of this matters or why you matter. Whatever the reason, you're now reading these pages. And that's a good thing because "Pick me up" also means *feeling better and finding ways to pick yourself up*. For example, you might be in the dumps and need a positive message to reset your thoughts and feelings.

The chapters in this book are based on my own personal playlist of positive, uplifting songs, and the tools I acquired to make it through my own journey. You'll see song titles heading each chapter (some familiar or perhaps unfamiliar) to inspire you to create a playlist or randomly listen in. I recommend listening to each of the songs mentioned in each chapter so you get a feel for how they helped me navigate life's ups and downs. You can search for these songs on Google, Spotify, or YouTube. Some YouTube videos even display the lyrics. There are several applicable approaches and techniques you can use while evoking wonderful musical tunes and lyrics–either my choices or your own. You'll always find beneficial exercises and tips for picking up yourself at the end of each chapter.

There are great adventures ahead, so I suggest you get a notepad, sit back, and reflect on where you are heading through the pages ahead. I hope this "Pick Me Up" book makes a difference. If I can reach just one individual and impact a life, my goal has been met.

Enjoy!

CHAPTER 1

Music Feels Better with You

Music has got me through my life's best and worst moments. For years, my love for music has made the difference between a good day, an okay day, and a difficult day. What kind of music? Any kind of music. Take, for instance, the song "Music Sounds Better With You" by Big Time Rush (2011). As the upbeat musical notes and lyrics sink in, we become transfixed and transformed. I suppose you could say that music is transcendent. It triggers brain chemicals and modulates levels of dopamine (and feelings of pleasure).

Neurons fire with the beats of music. We experience personal joy whether listening alone or with others. In groups, it helps us feel connected as our brainwaves sync together.

Music also has a calming effect. It can slow our heart rate, deepen our breathing, and lower stress hormones. Awe, wonder, and other positive emotions tend to spark whether we are in our living rooms, at a concert, or in church.

When I was approximately five years old, we went to my great-grandmother's house on Sundays and had what was called "sing-ins." We sang hymns while a grown-up played on my great-grandmother's upright piano, built in the 1800s. Little did I know at the time that this piano would change my life. I had a burning desire, even at five years old, to pull up to the rows of black and white keys and play (or what I thought at the time was playing.) I banged around on it because I already knew the hymns and could sing them in my head. Somehow, I figured out how to make the keys work to match the song. What I realized was the more that I heard the words in my head, the more I could play the piano.

One notable thing to mention is that I only played on the right side of the keyboard. Oh, how I wished back then that I could play with both hands on the left and right side, but I just didn't know how.

The most fantastic thing happened to me when I was about six years old, which inspired this book. My great-grandmother asked if I would like to have her piano. My first experience of truly knowing love was with this old piano. I went to school every day and came home to play. If only I knew how to play both sides. If I had a difficult day during my elementary school years and my friends were being mean or faced problems in class or on the playground, there was pure joy waiting at home. Sitting at the piano and playing chased away my worries. It helped that I had quite the imagination. I could be anyone I wanted to be. This was the magic of that old piano. I could get away from it all. This is what got me through the day and how I learned to love music.

Junior high arrived, and all the trials and tribulations that come with adolescence hit me. As long as I was sitting at the piano, I could still be somebody, and it would get me through my day. Funny that an inanimate object would have that kind of effect on me. Through many trials and tribulations of adolescence, I found my solace in going to the piano. It was an escape and made my difficult days better. I thank God that my great-grandmother knew I needed a special friend.

As life would have it, I went to college, and I paid less and less attention to my old friend, the piano. Several years later, I got married and took the piano with me. I played on occasion, but it became substituted with kids, husband, work, and life in general. However, when I was having a difficult day, I would go and play the piano, and it would be there for me. I still could forget worries, and it always helped me to feel better.

So, this is the foundation of my love of music. It could turn a dreadful day into a good one. It lifted the mood on the darkest of days. It put a pep in my step and picked me up. Oh, by the way, I had a friend teach me a few of the basic chords on the left side of the piano, which really improved my skills.

CHAPTER 2
Backpack, Backpack

This book is full of backpack analogies. Why? Because life is a journey. We are all on one. No matter your age, you are on a path that leads to experiences of every kind. Everyone needs essential tools to help them along–and a place to pack and unpack them.

Consider the simplicity of Dora the Explorer's **"Backpack Backpack"** tune. As a parent or grandparent, you may have sung the lyrics with your kiddos: "I'm the backpack loaded up with things and knickknacks, too. Anything that you might need, I got inside for you."

What a great theme for this chapter! When you pick something up, oftentimes, you need a place to store it. A backpack, even an imaginary one, is critical for storing all our tools and pulling them out at the right time you need them most. Even metaphorically, you can begin storing essential tools in your backpack at any age, and the older you get, the more sophisticated the essentials will become.

As we go through life, we begin to acquire tools that are age appropriate. For example, in elementary school, we learn to sit still, follow instructions, and play with friends. We take these instructions and place them in our imaginary backpack for use later in life.

As adolescence hits and our brains and bodies develop, we begin to acquire additional tools for our backpack that we will need on the journey. For example, appearance becomes important as we begin to compare ourselves to our friends. Hair and makeup might be tools females need to help them feel worthwhile or valued. Males begin to acquire tools such as becoming stronger and faster.

As high school and college arrive, tools change once again, and we continue to load our backpacks even more. Metaphorically, tools such as self-acceptance, self-esteem, wit, etc. might become important to have in our backpack.

Although everyone's journey is different, we are all headed for a destination. There are essential tools that we need to be successful when embarking on our journey in life. At the end of this chapter, I list the essentials I needed for my journey, and you'll find your essentials might be different from mine. As you read along, you'll see how relevant these essentials can be on YOUR journey.

Although the essentials listed below are metaphorical in nature, they were my basics. The important thing to remember while reviewing these essentials is no matter your age, you'll continue to add to your repertoire and use what you need at the time you need it.

A backpack. One of the most important items to acquire is a backpack. Mine was imaginary, and I pretended to carry all the tools I needed for my journey. Music was so important to me growing up that I learned early on that my imaginary backpack needed to contain varieties of music that I could pull out and listen to help me along the way…much like the old piano.

A GPS/map. A GPS/map tells you where you are going and gives instructions on how to get there. Although imaginary, this guided my thoughts, philosophies, and the direction I was heading. I oftentimes would stop and think about where I currently found myself in life and where I was heading.

A compass. This tells you which direction you are going, and as life will have it, many times, I found myself switching or changing directions to adjust to the expectations/changes that happened in my life at various stages.

A cellphone light or flashlight. You never know when your light will get dimmed or darkness will happen; therefore, a light will help you see. There were times in my journey when I felt as though I could not clearly see the path I was headed. A light provided clarity and a sense of where I was going.

Scissors. Often, you will need something sharp to help you cut through the problems along the way that you encounter on your journey. My life's journey contained many obstacles that would arise, and pretending I could cut through those problems and hit them head-on helped me to navigate the many obstacles that I experienced along my path. Believe me, if you are reading these pages, there will be obstacles, and you will need something to get you through them.

As mentioned above, you will develop your own set of essentials for your backpack to help you navigate life no matter your age.

There are many benefits of looking at life like a journey such as satisfaction, achievements, monetary rewards, and the hope of a better life and future. You will find that as you end one journey, another one begins, which requires new tools to carry you along the next path.

As I took off to new uncertain territories, I oftentimes found my backpack getting overloaded and worn out. I considered acquiring a new backpack that could handle any new essentials. Oftentimes, zippers get stuck, and I certainly did not want to lose any of those essentials that I had already accumulated for my journey that were found useful.

You might find today, with so many choices, it's difficult to decide the best backpack for your new journey. Make sure you choose wisely—and choose one that holds all the essentials you'll need. Select one that has enough room to allow others to give you direction and help you stay on the right path, one that includes a light to help you see, a pocket for something sharp to cut through the barriers and obstacles that get in your way, and one that can hold a GPS/map and compass to guide your travels.

Now that you know the importance music played in my journey and have an idea of the essentials I needed for my backpack, I suggest you settle back and enjoy the chords of this journey.

CHAPTER 3
We Are Family

How many times do families need to be picked up? Similar to picking up a hairbrush to style our hair, the members of our families, at times, need a pick-me-up. **"We Are Family"** is a song recorded by American vocal group Sister Sledge, reaching number one on the Billboard Dance Club songs back in 1979. This song is about **YOU!** Wherever you are on your life's journey, there is someone **YOU** can call family. You don't even have to be related to the person. This song reflects that we are all in this together. We are all on the journey called life.

Who do you have that you can call family? Family doesn't have to be your parents, your siblings, or your relatives. It can be someone you connected with just today. Someone who stopped and took a few minutes to see you and hear you. Someone who made you feel valued and worthwhile, even for a second. Was it a teacher? Possibly a salesclerk? Maybe even the mail carrier?

I was blessed with a wonderful family; however, I had a teacher who "noticed" me first in junior high art class when I won first place for my toothpick creation. This was a school where I felt like a small fish in a big lake. I had never really "beat anyone out before" in much of anything; therefore, this was a big deal. Once I won, I connected with the teacher. This honor that was bestowed on me made me feel "good enough" in a huge school, where I very much did not stand out.

I won the great prize of a candy bar, which was no big deal; however, to be recognized for something that I did on my own was a big deal. The recognition from the art teacher meant more to me than the candy bar. Lesson learned: it feels good when someone recognizes something you do well, no matter your age. Shove this in the **backpack—recognition**. This made me feel good about my accomplishment, no matter how small it was.

When was the first time you ever remember being recognized or rewarded? How old were you? Think back to this experience, write it down, grab a hold of the memory, and place it in your backpack. You might need it later, and this memory can be pulled out at any time.

In a world of incivility, where people seldom stop and acknowledge others, the obligation must be upon us, you and I, to stop and recognize others. We cannot expect others to do this. So many people are starving for attention, which simply can be a wave or glance of acknowledgment by others. You can't wait for this to happen. We all need it too badly, and we need it NOW. We need to give recognition, and we need to receive recognition. This was a tool that should have been put in our backpacks long ago when we were young. It's the art of recognizing others–some people get it, and some do not. It's about stopping what one is doing and acknowledging someone else. Little children are starved for someone to notice them or something they do. They need recognition much more than stuff.

My own experience reminds me of a special uncle who "recognized" me when I was a small child. Even though my brother and I were just kids, it was important to me to be allowed to play a game of croquet with the adults in the backyard. It was not a big deal, but to an eight-year-old child, playing with the grownups was huge. This experience made me want to be competitive and win. I wanted to try my hardest for that special uncle who took a chance and allowed the kids to join in. Can you recall a similar experience?

You may remember, when growing up, someone waved from a car, which automatically triggered a wave back whether you knew the others or not. Where has this gone, and will we ever get this back? This gesture was taught to me at an early age. I shoved it in my backpack. Even today, I wave at someone who pulls over for me on the highway and allows me to pass. In today's world, it can also be considered dangerous. What a shame.

As humans, we are meant to be connected to one another, and we are meant to be physically touched by others. For example, Harry Harlow, an American psychologist, conducted psychological studies on rhesus monkeys during the '50s and '60s regarding attachment.

Specifically, Dr. Harlow placed newborn rhesus monkeys in cages, where they had access to two surrogate mothers–one made from wire, and one made out of terry cloth. Both surrogates had access to a baby bottle, which was attached. The monkeys developed an attachment to the cloth surrogate. Results indicated that bodily contact with the cloth provided comfort. Further results suggested that even when other things were placed in the cage, if the cloth surrogate wasn't there, the monkeys huddled in a corner and cried. When the cloth surrogate was present, they clung to it. Touch and being connected to something are important.

Who, today, are you connected with—a friend, a companion, a significant other? Who can you call family? Everybody needs somebody. You must take the initiative to find **YOUR** person, **YOUR** family, whoever it is. Someone to hear you and accept you as you are. You don't even have to spend a lot of time with that person. Just simply someone who validates you when you see them. Someone who accepts you for who you are.

I recently read that it's important as you age to ask your friends or family what they need from you. Do you need a hug, a listening ear, a non-judgmental attitude? Tell them what you need. It might make a difference in your day. We must get accustomed to "going after" what we need. If you need a listening ear, ask for it. If they say no, go ask someone else. This will provide you with the communication and feedback you need.

"We are Family" reminds me of the old saying, "Birds of a feather flock together," thus the geese story. Have you ever heard of the geese story? "Lessons from Geese" was transcribed from a speech given by Angeles Arrien at the (1991) Organizational Development Network and was based on the work of Milton Olson. Basically, geese fly in a V formation. Have you ever wondered why? As each bird flaps its wings, it creates an uplift for the bird immediately following. By flying in "V" formation, the whole flock adds at least seventy-one percent greater flying range than if each bird flew on its own.

Tool for the **backpack**: "Share a **common direction**." Get where you are going more quickly and easily by traveling on the thrust of one another." Again, we are meant to be connected to each other.

Now, this is the important part of the story. When a goose falls out of formation, it suddenly feels the drag and resistance of trying to go it alone and quickly gets back into formation to take advantage of the lifting power of the bird in front. Tool for the **backpack**: "Stay in formation with those people who are **headed the same way** we are." This is our family. Again, we are meant to be connected to each other. We should be willing to accept help and to give our help to others.

The geese story goes on to tell us that when the head goose gets fatigued, it rotates back in the wing, and another goose flies point. Tool for the **backpack**: "Take turns doing demanding jobs and **share the load**." We all get tired, discouraged, and feel unvalued. When this happens, it is important to get out of line and go back to your person to get encouraged and recharged. For me, music made me feel better. For you, it could be your person. It could be your dog. We all need to share each other's burdens.

The end of the geese story says that geese honk from behind to encourage those up front to keep up their speed. Tool for the **backpack: encouragement**, especially when we are leading the pack. We need to make sure our honking is encouraging. There is power in being in a group or with like-minded people who need encouragement. Encouragement helps us persist and keep moving forward. Lastly, when a goose gets sick or wounded, two geese drop out of formation and follow it down to help and protect it. They stay with it until it dies or can fly again. Then, they launch out with another formation or catch up with the flock. The lesson here is we need to **stand by each other** in challenging times, as well as when we are strong.

The story of the geese flying in a "V" formation is definitely a tool that I suggest you place in your **backpack**. Over the years, I have pulled this out numerous times when I needed encouragement or lost my way. I have applied this story to my adult life many times throughout my career. As a counselor, I pulled out various tools from this story and shared them with my students, who felt they were alone or just could not go on.

As a teacher, I pulled it out when students weren't grasping a concept in class or lost interest. I reminded them that we were a team and in this together. I reminded them that their success in my class was my success. As an administrator, I pulled out many of the concepts of the geese story when employees lost their way, lost their enthusiasm, or lost their passion for their work.

Another essential tool for your **backpack** from the song **"We are Family"** is **GOALS**. No matter if you are a child, a teenager, an adult, or elderly, we all need goals. They need to be within our reach, and we need to have faith in ourselves that we can accomplish them. As a child, your goal for the day might be to do your chores or go to school and do your best. If you are elderly, your goal may be to get up, make yourself presentable, and do one productive thing for the day.

One of my daily goals, which is a daily prayer, is to bless at least one person every day. I never know who it is going to be; however, at the end of the day, I reflect on anyone I encountered who I might have helped or blessed. Goals do not have to be lengthy. Just attainable.

It's okay to change your goals. Oftentimes, as life gets in the way, we change our minds. I never set my goal to be a college teacher, counselor, or administrator. It just happened, and I kept changing my short-term goals to help me reach where I was going. Rest assured; it is okay to change your goals. Goals are essential throughout our entire lives and will change as we age. For young people, your goal might be to finish school and go to college. For others, to be a good parent, wife, and husband.

For the elderly, to work at being healthy, reading more, etc. You get the point. Goals are essential. They must be realistic, and they must be shared with an accountability partner that will help you stay on task. You also must believe in YOU. You must be okay with starting over again. This is all part of life.

Backpack tool: Goals—and change them as you age.

"We are Family" has meant so much to me over the years. In all of my career positions, I've sought out my people who became my family. We shared common goals and picked each other up. This was most apparent as a college administrator. My team was my family. My college employees were my family, my faculty were my family. My students were my family.

EXERCISE (GOALS)

Take out a sheet of paper and fold it in half.

1. Write down what you want to be when you grow up. If you are already grown up, write down what you would like to be late in life. A writer, an artist, a singer, a nurse, or a friend to someone?

2. Write down what you can do within the next three months to accomplish your goal. For example, take an art class. It could be to save up the money for three months, research art lessons, or get enrolled in a class.

3. Write down what you can do within one year to accomplish this goal. For example, another art class, or reading books on art, etc.

4. Write down what you can do within five years to accomplish this goal. For example, maybe you are now teaching art; how can you continue to grow and learn about art to help your students?

5. Now on the blank upper part of the paper. Draw what you want to be or print/cut out a picture of

what you want to be or do. For example, if it is a nurse, draw or cut out a picture of a nurse and tape it to your paper.

6. Place the picture on your refrigerator where you will see it every day. This is to remind you of where you are headed, just like a compass.

7. Share this with someone you know who will hold you accountable for completing your goal. Telling family or a friend what you are trying to accomplish will help you stay focused on the goal and help you hold yourself accountable.

BACKPACK TOOLS FROM CHAPTER 3

RECOGNITION

COMMON DIRECTION

SAME DIRECTION AS OTHERS

SHARE THE LOAD

ENCOURAGEMENT

GOALS

You may have to pull out the GPS/map and compass and let your family know where you are heading. Your flashlight might be needed on occasion to be able to see ahead where you are going, and do not forget the scissors. You might need to cut through the obstacles or problems along the way. Yes, we are all family. We need to stick together. If we do, this just might **change the world**.

CHAPTER 4
Change the World

For others to see who we really are, we oftentimes need a pick-me-up, a boost, a shove, a push, etc. The song "If I Could Change the World" picks me up. Singer and songwriter Eric Clapton recorded the song, and I am in love with blues music. In fact, this artist is one of my favorite musicians.

"If I Could Change the World" was written by Tommy Sims, Gordon Kennedy, and Wayne Kirkpatrick. It was released on July 5, 1996. Eric Clapton recorded the song for John Travolta's movie, *Phenomenon*. As president of a community college for eight years, I used this song as a theme at the beginning of a school year with the intention of emphasizing no matter what your position is in life, you can change the world. This song is another one that is written specifically for **YOU!** No matter what age or stage of life you are in, you have the capacity to make a difference to others.

I encourage you to play this song several times and listen to the words. Basically, this indicates to me that we need to take off our masks and our facades and peel the onion back, if you will. Inside of an onion, once the layers have been peeled away, is a core or middle. Similar to an onion, within our inner core lies our insecurities, pains, and hurts. Why are we so afraid to let people, even the ones we are closest to see who we really are on the inside? I believe it is because we are afraid of what they might see our insecurities, our fears, and our pain.

What are you hiding in your core being that is keeping you from being who you were intended to be? Why is it so difficult to be our true, authentic selves?

We have love in our hearts for specific people, friends, and family; however, we sometimes hide behind baggage, hurts, pain, and insecurities that we do not want others to know exist.

As this was written as a love song, it has so many implications for more than one special person. Using this song, I challenged my faculty and staff to make a difference, even if it was only for one student.

An example of this, at the beginning of a school year, I coined the phrase, "Each One Reach One." I challenged my faculty and staff during one specific semester to take the time to put all their energies and efforts into at least one student to make a difference for that semester. In other words, give more attention than usual to a student that they felt truly needed something from them.

A good example of this is a true story of an experience I had upon being selected as the president of the college. As was customary on most days, I was usually one of the last employees to leave the campus at the end of the day. On one particular Friday, on which we close at 4 pm, I locked my office and headed to the parking lot toward my car. I looked around the parking lots and didn't see any other vehicles. As I cranked my car, I noticed a car pulling up in front of the administration building. I watched to see what happened next. After sitting in her car for what seemed quite a bit of time, a young lady opened the door and headed up the hill to the administration building front door.

I knew the door would be locked because we were closed, and everyone had left for the weekend. Now, keep in mind that this was the Friday before classes began for a new term on Monday. Late registration was over, and we were ready to begin a new term. Also, it is relevant to mention that I was worn out. Physically exhausted from a very tedious week, where we encountered some technological difficulties during the week. I could not wait to get the weekend started.

After observing the young lady, who slowly began to head to the front door, I got out of my car and walked around to the front of the building and met her. I asked if I could help. She indicated that she was there to register for classes. I informed her that the college was closed for the weekend and would not open until Monday and that late registration was over. The look on her face tugged at my heartstrings. She said okay and began to walk away.

As she turned away, I asked her to remain there and let me go to the car and get a piece of paper. I asked her if she had completed admission paperwork and had been assessed, to which she replied, "No." I asked if she had any idea what type of courses she was interested in, and she grinned with a smile I will never forget. She said, "Nursing."

I explained that nursing was a select program for which she would have to meet specific requirements for entrance and to be accepted into the program; however, there were prerequisites she could take. I took down her information and told her I would have someone call her first thing Monday morning to get the ball rolling to get her admitted, assessed, and enrolled.

She thanked me in a way I will never forget, simply the expression of gratitude on her face still flashes in my mind. Fast forward, she got enrolled and began taking her prerequisites for the nursing program.

As president of the college, it is customary at the end of the year to attend the nursing pinning ceremony and congratulate the graduates. For the president, it is one of the most memorable occasions, although I usually did not recognize or know all the students. At the reception, many siblings, spouses, and parents attend, and many pictures are taken.

At this particular ceremony, suddenly, a young woman came up to me and asked if she could have a picture with me. I agreed. She asked if I recognized her, and I told her I thought she looked familiar but could not place her. She proceeded to remind me that she was the young lady who showed up at the building after closing hours a year ago, and I helped her get enrolled.

Then I recognized her. She said if it were not for me, she would not have had her dream come true to be a nurse. She told me that I was her hero and had changed her life. She preceded to tell me that what I did not know was that she had made three previous trips to the campus, which was over an hour from her home, to get enrolled and was afraid that she wasn't good enough nor smart enough to go to nursing school; therefore, all three times she drove away without getting out of her car. She said she finally got the courage to get out of her car and walk to the door, only to find it locked.

She then said, "You were like an angel that showed up out of nowhere and helped me." While decked out in her uniform of white, she proceeded to say, "Look at me now!" With tears flowing, I hugged her and told her how proud I was of her. She said she was a single parent with three kids and was trying to provide a better life for her family. She then asked me my name and what I did at the college. I told her I was the president. She said, "No way." Wow! You never know the influence you have on others or how just what one little thing can possibly change lives forever. I was tired from a long week but took the time to help her. Look at the results.

There is a lot of room in your backpack for getting beyond

yourself to help others. I cannot tell you how I felt seeing how this frightened, shy young lady had blossomed into a confident, beautiful nurse decked out in her uniform. You see, we never know the baggage that people carry with them. I had no idea that she had already been to the college three times and got scared and went back home. I had no idea that she was a single parent trying to better her life for her children.

You can CHANGE the WORLD!

It only takes one.

First Lady Eleanor Roosevelt comes to mind as someone who made a difference. She exemplifies the epitome of going "beyond herself" to help others. For example, she was known for making great strides in advocating for the rights of women, as well as minorities in the United States back in the '30s and '40s. She got beyond herself to promote women's rights in the workplace and raised funds for the Women's Trade Union League to raise the minimum wage, end child labor, and promote health and safety regulations in the workplace. One of her most notable causes was establishing a school for girls and promoting education for young girls, and she was an outspoken critic of racial discrimination. The remarkable contributions of First Lady Roosevelt came during one of the worst crises in American history—the Great Depression.

No matter your walk in life, no matter your age or where you are on your own personal journey, **YOU** can make a difference every day to someone else. When you find yourself in the darkest of days, reach inside your backpack, and then reach out to do something for someone else; you will feel better, and it will pick you up.

When you are at your worst, feel depressed, or feel

unworthy, then get beyond yourself and change the world for a family member, a friend, a neighbor, or even better, someone you don't even know.

Here is another good example. I was having a pity party one day for some strange reason. I seldom ever get down, but this specific day, I was low. I went to the grocery store to get some things quickly. An elderly lady was in front of me and taking forever. I could feel myself getting impatient. She began to pull out her coupons, which took even longer. As I waited, the clerk told her what she owed. She emptied her purse out and did not have enough money to pay for her groceries. She began trying to decide what to put back, which took even longer. The line behind me began to grow, and people were becoming impatient and grumbling.

Suddenly, something came over me, and I asked the clerk how much she was short. She indicated $21.00. I reached into my purse and paid the bill. The lady began thanking me and blessing me for what I had done. I walked away feeling very satisfied that I helped someone out, and I thanked God for the opportunity to be able to help her. I went home with an entirely new mindset and finished the day feeling happy. I was blessed.

This is so simple to do. The blessing I received meant much more to me than the money. Even if one is not capable of solving another's problem, there are still ways to be helpful. You can call a neighbor and check-in, you can bring in a neighbor's trash can or newspaper, or you can go to the nursing home and read to someone who is lonely. There are so many opportunities to change the world. It starts with the right attitude and a willing heart. This is what our backpacks are meant for, and you can pull it out anytime you are feeling low. Sometimes, you simply have to give others something, even when they don't know what they need. We all have the ability to change the world in small and large ways.

You may not even realize the difference you have made or the influence you've had on others for years to come. Trust me. It will come back to you at some point in your life. An interesting way this has come back to me is when I was a vice president at the college. On occasion, before the end of the semester, I would get tired and worn out and begin to contemplate if I was doing the Lord's work. Sometimes, days would become ho-hum, mundane, etc., especially when I was the most fatigued. I did not get this way often, however, when I did, I would get pretty low. It never failed that a former student called or stopped by to see me, usually one that I hadn't seen or heard from in several years.

One specific day, a former baseball player stopped by and asked to see me. I barely remembered him, as I had seen many baseball players enter and exit my office frequently. He assumed that I remembered him, never gave me his name, but rather proceeded to ask me if I remembered when he barged into my office and told me he was quitting school and quitting baseball.

I said, "No, I don't recall that situation." He reminded me that I stopped what I was doing, got out of my chair, and marched him all the way across campus back to his class while preaching all the way that he was not quitting school and that I insisted that he make something of himself. I asked his name, and we figured out together that it had been five years since that moment, and he wanted me to know that he graduated with his master's degree and was going to work on his doctorate degree. He said if I hadn't insisted that he go back to class and keep working hard, he would not be where he is today. He thanked me, we shook hands, and off he went.

Each one, reach one! Yep, days like these always solidified that I was doing the Lord's work.

Our hearts are hidden by pain, hurt, baggage, and life. How do we get about the business of being "real and genuine?" How do we peel back the layers to let others really see who we are? I believe it starts with laying down our insecurities and taking a risk of being okay with letting others see who we are. It starts with letting go of the fear of being judged. It takes risk-taking. What is the worst that can happen?

It could be that someone doesn't like us or actively works against us, which happens sometimes. While we might not win everyone over, I believe there is someone we can win over if we keep trying, keep being genuine and willing to let others see us for who we are. They might like the real you. They might learn something in the process of your "letting go" and begin to peel back their own layers.

Backpack essential: risk-taking to strip off the masks you wear. Let people see the real you. Each one, reach one, and it only takes one.

Have you ever heard of the starfish story? The starfish story was adapted from "*The Star Thrower*" by Loren C. Eiseley, copyright 1968. It goes like this:

> "A young girl was walking along a beach upon which thousands of starfish had been washed up during a terrible storm. When she came to each starfish, she picked it up and threw it back into the ocean. People watched her with amusement.
>
> She had been doing this for some time when a man approached her and said, 'Little girl, why are you doing this? Look at this beach! You cannot save all these starfish. You cannot begin to make a difference!' The girl seemed crushed and suddenly deflated. After a few moments, she bent down, picked up another starfish, and hurled it as far as she

could into the ocean. Then she looked up at the man and replied, 'Well, I made a difference for that one!'

The old man looked at the girl inquisitively and thought about what she had done. Inspired, he joined the little girl in throwing starfish back into the sea. Soon, others joined, and all the starfish were saved."

You can make a difference to one.

EXERCISE (EACH ONE REACH ONE)

Select one person per month to place most of your attention. Provide acts of kindness during the month to that person:

1. Send a "thinking of you" card.

2. Take them food or a snack.

3. Ask them to go to a movie or event.

4. Compliment the individual or give them positive feedback.

5. Honor a rite of passage, e.g., birthday, anniversary, etc.

6. Ask the individual to come to your house.

7. Offer to be a mentor to that individual.

8. Go walking/running together for a cause.

EXERCISE (THE SELF)

Take out three pieces of paper.

1. In ten or fewer words, describe your "actual self."
    How do you currently see yourself?
    Example: teacher, father, employee.

2. In ten or fewer words, describe your "ought self."
    These are beliefs you have about yourself and the
    duties and obligations you have.
    Example: Pay taxes, vote.

3. In ten or fewer words, describe your "ideal self."
    These are words that describe your hopes, wishes,
    and aspirations. Example: Travel to a foreign
    country, coach little league, sing in a choir.

4. Which self are you striving for? How can you reach
    your authentic self?

Anxiety and frustration come when our different "selves" are incongruent and become in conflict with each other.

BACKPACK TOOLS FROM CHAPTER 4

EACH ONE, REACH ONE

RISK-TAKING

Letting go and offering myself to others is freeing and brings *joy to my heart*.

CHAPTER 5

Joy in My Heart

An absolute must for your **backpack** is making space for **joy**. Joy gives the pick-me-up we all need. Listening to the song "Joy In My Heart" is a must. It can bring you out of a funk. It can pick you up! The lyrics to "Joy in My Heart" were written by George William Cooke and released on January 1, 1925.

So, what is this thing called "joy," and how does this bring value to me? Joy is defined in Webster's Dictionary as "the emotion evoked by well-being, success, or good fortune or by the prospect of possessing what one desires." Theopedia describes it more convincingly as "a state of mind and an orientation of the heart."

If "joy" is a state of mind and an orientation of the heart, how do we arrive at that state? What do we have to do to get there? Do we wake up having joy in our hearts? It takes action on our part. For me, I must work at it. Not every day is a good day. There are days that we wake up feeling blue for a variety of reasons. The loss of a loved one, a bad grade, unacceptance into a group or club, etc. With so much negativity in our world today and the past pandemic, which affected the health and well-being of people we love, we were all challenged to find some type of delight, happiness, and normalcy in our lives.

Where can we find joy in the midst of things not being

okay for us? Over the last few years, the word "joy" has taken on a new meaning for me. Being the optimist that I am, I believe that good things come out of bad situations. Oftentimes, I don't go looking for joy, but rather, joy seems to find me.

An example of this came a couple of years ago. I was on an international trip to Europe with students. Upon traveling many roads and visiting many villages and towns in Europe, I was reminded of all the conveniences and freedoms we are provided in America. A simple observation was that not all toilets in the world had seats or lids, and not everyone had a toilet. Not all the roads in the world are paved and convenient to drive on.

This observation caused me to reflect on having joy in my heart and thankfulness for the blessings and freedoms that we have in America. Upon the final days of my trip and the urgency to get home, I found myself dealing with flight cancellations, screenings, and customs checks. While I could have been frustrated, I found joy in this experience. Despite the chaos, witnessing the patience that people had with each other at the airports and the airport attendants going out of their way to get us home brought joy to my heart.

During this experience of international travel, my most memorable moment ensued upon walking into the U.S. Customs area and hearing the workers saying, "Welcome back home to the USA." This was music to my ears. Joy definitely has a new meaning to me in my life.

As a president, leading a college through a pandemic was another experience where joy found me. This could have been the worst time of my life in administration. I had never been through a pandemic nor ever dreamed that I'd be running a college during a pandemic. Leading a college remotely and ensuring the safety and security of our students, faculty, and staff, once back on campus, became my priority. Joy filled my heart to see the college family come together and work diligently to ensure our students were our priority, making sure they were taken care of and had the tools they needed to transition to remote learning.

Often, in dark times and tragedies, you'll find neighbors helping each other and people coming together to assist each other. For example, when I was young, my home was destroyed by a tornado. What I witnessed was people bringing food and clothing and offering shelter to those who had lost their homes. I took this experience as a wake-up call for us to get off the roller coaster, appreciate what we have, and love and support those around us. This is a reason to be joyful.

Joy needs to be in the **backpack**. You don't always have to go looking for joy, but rather be open to letting it find you. All we are promised is right here, right now. Let joy be a part of right here, right now.

Although it is refreshing for joy to find us, we are required to do something to continually maintain joy. This takes work. For me, I wake up each day with the mindset that I'm going to have joy in my heart. This is critical in determining what type of day I will experience.

Remember, action is required on our part. It's unnatural unless joy accidentally finds us. I was raised that if someone does something for you, you pay it forward by doing something for someone else. Growing up, I observed my family "exchange" items with one another for no reason. In other words, if someone brought food to my house, we would not let them leave without them accepting something in return.

Joy in your heart can be the simplest of things, such as waving in gratitude for someone pulling over to let you by in your car. Isn't this common courtesy? Why do we see fewer and fewer people showing attitudes of gratitude?

Can we always have joy in our hearts? There will be days

when this is just not possible; however, searching for something joyful during our day that we can hold onto might just be the answer.

Joy is a learned behavior. We are not born to have joy in our hearts. We learn this at an early age from those around us. We observe it and watch it in those around us and on television. Is it too late to develop joy in our hearts? My answer is, "No." As in the fitness world, you cannot practice lifting weights once and develop muscles. It takes consistent and intentional lifting. Similarly, you must monitor your attitude, check your heart, and practice having joy with intentionality.

Having joy in your heart might be contagious. Work at it consistently by practicing joyfulness every day. This is a choice, and it takes practice. Take my friend, Scotty, one of those people who always makes you feel good to be around. Although our paths do not cross frequently, when they do, I always come away blessed. Recently, Scotty lost his spouse and soulmate of fifty years, who had been battling a terminal illness.

For several days, I kept thinking about the joy that Scotty radiates whenever anyone is around him and how unsettling it would be to see him lose that joy through the loss of a loved one. I made a special point to go by to see him, and express my condolences, and to my amazement, Scotty was no different than any other day I stopped by. I left once again being blessed by my friend, who, although grieving, had the uncanny ability to make me feel better leaving than when I arrived, even in his time of despair.

Place joy in your backpack and keep joy in your heart.

EXERCISE (JOURNAL)

A good exercise to try:

Keep a joy in your heart journal. Write down three things per day for which you are grateful and have joy in your heart. Go back and review the journal at the end of the week.

Develop the mindset that you are going to build a joy muscle. Work on it consistently, just like lifting weights and building muscle.

EXERCISE (MASON JAR)

1. Take a mason jar, cut a slit in the top, and every day that you catch yourself feeling joyful, drop a nickel, a dime, or quarter in the jar.

2. Check your jar at the end of the month and donate your funds to the charity of your choice, which will bring additional joy!

BACKPACK TOOLS FROM CHAPTER 5

JOY IN YOUR HEART

SEND A CARD OR TEXT TO SOMEONE WHO IS LONELY OR ILL

CALL A FRIEND

THANK SOMEONE

Having joy in your heart will prevent you from focusing on "I." It will move the emphasis from you to others. There are so many ways to show gratitude, which will bring you joy. Remember, "What I tend to be totally begins with me." The small act of having joy in your heart might cause you to **celebrate the good times** in your life.

accomplishing or receiving recognition, good for you. This is a reason to celebrate.

I have been attending graduation ceremonies for almost 40 years, and my cup runneth over with pride and joy in knowing that I just might have had some little something to do with the celebration. Even if you encourage someone to start a new health plan, this is a reason to celebrate. You must look for reasons to celebrate every day. Just the fact that you meet your friends, family, or strangers, whatever their walks in life, and encourage them to start something new or congratulate them on something they have done is a reason to celebrate. You may have just been the one person who was with them on their journey of self-exploration to find themselves.

Celebrating can also require preparation and work. You might be asked to help decorate, send out invitations, or assist with food. The excitement begins just with the announcement of a celebration.

I always made it a point at the end of the spring semester near graduation to walk over to the Enrollment Management Department because that is where our students picked up their caps and gowns for the graduation ceremony. When students pick up their cap and gown, a transformation takes place. There is simply no way to explain this. They rip open their cap and gown and try it on. They begin talking about and imagining themselves becoming a teacher, a nurse, a pilot. They can be whoever they want to be. The party has begun.

The pride that comes with the celebration is not just for the recipients of the degree. If you have had even one thing to do to help with the success of someone, there are reasons for you to celebrate. For me, on the evening of graduation, I am continually amazed year after year to see a similar transformation in the faculty and staff who have worked with these students throughout the year. As students walk across the stage and receive their diplomas, I'm impressed to see faculty standing and cheering for those students that they recognize. Oftentimes, students will step out of line and walk over to the faculty member to give them a hug and offer gratitude for their help throughout the year.

This transformation is what I call a reciprocal relationship. The person that has helped is just as happy as the one who is being celebrated. This is why it is so important to place **celebration** in your **backpack**. You can pull it out at any time.

Serving as president, I was afforded the opportunity to confer the graduates their degrees. I always made it a point, in all the pomp and circumstance, as well as pageantry, to encourage the audience not to hold back but to yell out in celebratory fashion with cheers of joy how proud they are of their graduate. I encourage you to laugh, to have a party, and to celebrate. You need to take ownership of what you have done for others. Give it all you have, set your standards high, and expect the same effort for yourself.

No wonder there is such a party going on. Like any good party or celebration, sometimes a dance or reception occurs. This is the transition of you and the partygoers coming together to celebrate. You two are in a symbiotic relationship where each is dancing together at the party, where sometimes you lead and something your friend leads. During this dance, relationships build, respect is earned, and success manifests itself. Our commencement or graduation party does not end with the ceremony or party. It's just the beginning of a new dance, a new party with new participants who become a little more experienced and equipped to lead or follow in their next dance or celebration.

Listed below are some ways to celebrate **YOU** and any accomplishment! They can be altered to fit your preference:

EXERCISE (CELEBRATION)

1. Create a collage of pictures of the accomplishment you are celebrating and hang it in your house. Upon my retirement, I developed a scrapbook, which included many pictures of pleasant memories, awards, and accomplishments of our college.

2. Develop a wall of fame with certificates, awards, and pictures of your celebration.

3. Develop an office or special place at your home housing your trophies and awards.

4. To celebrate a life well lived, plant a tree in honor of someone else. Develop a butterfly garden in memory of someone special.

5. Do something out-of-the-ordinary that gives you a sense of sophistication. Every time you feel like celebrating, write your ideas down in a very nicely decorated binder with a fancy pen.

BACKPACK TOOLS FROM CHAPTER 6

CELEBRATION

PARTY

LAUGHTER

Tools for the **backpack: celebration, fun, party**. The relationships that I encountered during my celebrations will *stand by me* forever...

CHAPTER 7
Stand by Me

Being picked up by someone else or having someone stand by you picks you up. **"Stand by Me"** has always been one of my favorite songs, and after seeing the movie, which included the song, it became one of my kids' favorites. **"Stand by Me"** was written and released in 1961 by singer/songwriter Ben E. King along with Jerry Leiber and Mike Stoller. This is another great song written especially for **YOU!**

We all need someone to stand by us. No matter how tough life gets, it just seems more bearable when someone is sharing it with you. What a pick-me-up to know that someone is sharing my sorrows and pain. There are so many implications to this song, and so many tools for the backpack.

We, as human beings, are meant to be connected to others. We are not meant to go through life alone. Stop and think a minute about someone that you know right now, right this minute, who has your back. I bet everyone reading this book knows of someone. If you were stranded on an island by yourself and could have one person with you, who would it be? Who would you call your person?

Life is what I call a sense of community. According to *Webster's Dictionary*, "community" is defined as a unified body of individuals, such as people with common interests living in a particular area. This could be just one person we prefer to stand with. Over the years, I have seen so many new students enter our college doors, where families drop them off and tell them, "Good luck, and see you at Christmas."

They enter the college doors knowing no one; however, the most amazing thing happens within a noticeably brief period of time. They meet a friend.

A good example of this is a student from out of state. I happened to meet her on the first day on our campus. She was shy, withdrawn and inundated with feelings of awkwardness. She was full of dreams but needed that "someone" to stand by her and support her through the educational process. I cannot help but feel a sense of pride in knowing the sacrifices she had made to acquire her degree to become a nurse. As she walked off the graduation stage, I was pleasantly surprised to hear a cheering section coming from other students yelling, "Way to go, Ellen!" and "You did it!" In a very short amount of time, she had bonded with her nursing comrades.

Engaging learners as full partners in the learning process resembles the adage, "Two become one." Giving students a real-world experience by meeting other students and sharing in their world gives them the encouragement they need to move forward.

Then there is "Billy"—a special needs student who wanted an education in a small setting. Although he received plenty of support from his family, he wanted to live in our residential halls and acquire a feeling of independence. As he approached me on the stage to receive his diploma, he was grinning from ear to ear. Billy was one of those students with an infectious character, and this character overshadowed the fact he was a student with a disability.

I befriended Billy early on, and when he was down the most, he showed up at the end of the day to just visit. We created many options and opportunities for him to be successful. We paired him with another student in his field, and they became friends. Where Jack was insecure, Billy was confident, and vice versa. Billy not only graduated but landed his first job before leaving school. What I learned from him was giving the absolute best of yourself to others will help them blossom. His transformation was certainly apparent. I've been blessed to have had a career in the people business. I have stories after stories to tell of the successes of people because someone stood by them, whether it be a teacher, a family member, or a newfound friend.

Who do you have to stand with? Who will choose to stand by you? For me, I always preferred one-on-one with one other person. We all tend to pay more attention when we are the focus of one person's attention. As a kid, I'd rather play basketball one-on-one because I did not have to share the ball with others. As a student in school and needing help from a teacher, I seemed to work better when it was just the teacher and I instead of a group.

Part of our responsibility as adults is to ensure that others are not alone. We must take ownership of the fact that we have due diligence to make connections between people. Things like one-on-one talks with a friend or one-on-one story sharing with an advisor just seem to help others succeed. Oftentimes, bonds form that last a lifetime. Encouragement seems to be more meaningful when we are one-on-one.

Being **one-on-one with someone** was a useful tool for my **backpack** and maybe yours too. One of my favorite examples of this was meeting Phillip, an international student. He came to the U.S. to study and improve his English-speaking ability. He was a shy and immature student who had never been away from home. Phillip and I bonded right from the start. He latched on to me like a mother. I was his "person," and he proceeded to remind me of this often. Frequently, he would stop by my office to ask questions, which were usually about American customs.

He and I shared a love of fishing, and the next thing I knew, he caught a fish out of our campus pond. He barged into my office with the fish still on the pole and demanded I bring him a pan, utensils, and plate so he could cook the fish in his dorm room. Unfortunately, I had to hurry him out of my office to prevent the dripping fish from getting on my carpet, and I had to tell him that cooking in the residential halls was prohibited. However, we found a way to cook at the pond, and we both enjoyed conversation one-on-one over a very small plate of one fish. Although he graduated and returned to his country, he stayed in touch with me and made frequent calls to ask about "Texas slang." This is one-on-one at its best. I challenge you no matter where you are in your journey of life to find someone to be **one-on-one to stand by**. Your lives will be enriched. Another tool for the **backpack**.

As I close this chapter, I am reminded that sometimes we must go back to the basics and make life a little simpler. There is no better example of this than what we observe from children. They do one-on-one very well. They, better than adults, have lessons from which we can learn. For example, I am reminded of the words written by Robert Fulghum, author of *All I Really Need to Know I Learned in Kindergarten* (1986). If we are going to find a person to stand by, these words will hit home for you. This fits nicely as an exercise.

EXERCISE (ONE-ON-ONE)

- Share everything
- Play fair
- Don't hit people

- Put things back where you found them

- Clean up your own mess

- Don't take things that are not yours

- Say you are sorry when you hurt somebody

- Wash your hands

- Flush

- Warm cookies and cold milk are good for you

- Live a balanced life

- Learn some and think some

- And draw, paint, and sing and dance

- And play and work every day some

- Take a nap every afternoon

- When you go out into the world

- Watch out for traffic

- Hold hands and stick together

- Be aware of wonder

The line that jumps out to me is "Hold hands and stick together." I recently had the opportunity to pick up my four-year-old grandson from pre-k. Now, you must understand it has been years since I did something like this. I was somewhat nervous that I would not find him or that he would not find me due to being on the playground with many other kids. The first thing I noticed was when the bell rang and it was time to go, they all ran to find a friend, held hands, and walked out together.

Was this to keep them from running off? Was this to teach them discipline? Regardless, they all had their person, someone to stand with when exiting the playground and going out into the world. We all have someone. If you don't, get up, find him or her, and grab a hand.

Remember the chant, "Red rover, red rover, let Annie come over?" Another childhood chant was "Ring around the rosie, a pocket full of posies, ashes, ashes, we all fall down!" Have you ever noticed that these childhood chants we grew up with had more than one person in the rhyme? This is what made these games so much fun–the fact that those of us singing the tune were doing so with a partner. I enjoyed it so much when on the playground, a friend or teammate would run over to stand next to me after his/her name was called. We would all fall in the grass, rolling with laughter. Yes, we are meant to be connected to others.

Research confirms that people who feel connected to others have lower levels of depression and anxiety, higher self-esteem, and greater trust and empathy for others. When you have good news, you want to share it with someone. When you are upset or sad, there is nothing like someone to lean on. We are definitely stronger together. When we can put aside our differences, we are at our best. I take immense pride in and cherish each and every connection that I've made in the education field. Some of these connections have resulted in life-long friends. Some are community partners, who are the most reliable connections that support me. Your **backpack** has room for you to have a connection with someone.

BACKPACK TOOLS FROM CHAPTER 7

ONE-ON-ONE

CONNECTION TO SOMEONE

As a result of and because of the pandemic, Americans became disconnected from one another. Fear stymied our connectedness, causing isolation, loneliness, and depression. Despite our differences, and because of our differences, since the pandemic has waned, we have become connected again. When you have a connection, you are not alone. Your **backpack** has room for both of you, and if you choose to go it alone, it might end up in a *landslide*…

CHAPTER 8

Landslide

"Landslide" is a song written by one of my favorite female artists, Stevie Nicks. This was first performed by the group Fleetwood Mac and recorded in 1975. It was relevant to include this song to show that I'm not a <u>Pollyanna</u>—everything is not always okay. Sometimes, things fall apart. We all need to be picked up and carried some time in our lives. What I have learned over the years is that it is not the destination that is important but the journey along the way and how we manage the tough times, as well as the good.

This song speaks to me as it reflects that our lives are passing by, we are aging, and can we manage the changes that are coming even though we don't know what the changes are? Sometimes, what comes into our lives are total landslides, devastations, and tragedies. Do you have room in your backpack for something like this? Of course. You cannot appreciate the good times without having experienced some tough times. Landslides build character. I would not be where I am today without having experienced many landslides and failures.

We have undergone the most tumultuous times in the last few years with incivility in our country, as well as the pandemic and so many deaths. Hatred and anger are running rampant.

There is distrust, disrespect, and the discounting of human lives. You may ask yourself, What can little ol' me do to help our anguishing world? Don't you see, everything begins with "me," "you" and "us." You can begin by offering up something. This will give you the pick-me-up you need. You cannot give what you do not have, but you can offer up something.

As an American author and minister, Max Lucado (2014) states, "You can come with empty hands and high hopes." You can show support, show understanding, and be accepting of life as it comes. You can be better than you were the day before. You can make a difference in a small way. When a landslide comes-and believe me, no matter your age, it will come—you must rely on your morals, your values, your skills, and your relationships to get you through it.

Some tools for your **backpack** that can help are things like **empathy**, **sympathy**, and **compassion** for others. **Acceptance** and **understanding** are also good tools. One valuable tool is learning how to pick yourself up and reach out of your comfort zone to begin a new initiative or movement that betters yourself and others. Perhaps it is talking with others who have had similar landslides and offering a listening ear.

You might discover when the landslides come, you may have to dig deep in the bottom of the backpack to find the right tool you need. These tools you have had in your backpack often end up in the bottom, and they are hard to find. It not only takes searching to find them but practice, practice, and practice. As stated earlier, you cannot build muscles with one lift of a weight. You must lift repeatedly to build muscles.

I am here to tell you, do not get caught up in the hype, the media, and the drama of our world. Draw upon those simple tools that might be rusty and in the bottom of the backpack. Pull them out, dust them off, and use them repeatedly. When your landslide hits, pull yourself up and try to be better than the day before. Take a risk, a position, and stand up for what is right. Do not settle for the way things are in your life. Create real and sustainable change in yourself that is lasting and leaves the world a better place for all.

I am reminded of when I was walking my dog one day, and I noticed after a good rain that the weeds and tall grass were everywhere. This walk and looking at the weeds reminded me of the weeds I have in my own life. Do I have things in my life that I am allowing to "take over" my time instead of spending time with family? Do I ever feel myself "in the weeds?" When I was gardening, I learned quickly that if you do not pull the weeds while they are small, they will take over your garden and become harder to get out. They will oftentimes "choke" out your good plants.

Similar to the landslides in our lives, developing people is very much like weeding, managing, and growing a garden. Plants must be weeded, watered, fertilized, and pruned to produce the best harvest. People, as well as ourselves, are no different. Our best asset at any company or organization is our people. Our best asset at our schools is the students. They deserve the same guidance and care as plants in order to grow to their potential. If a landslide comes, and we are knocked down and covered by the weeds, there is always a way out.

We must be empowered to step out on our own with projects and tasks that give us freedom to succeed or fail. In times of failure, you have to permit yourself particular care and attention, just like keeping the plants weeded and watered. We oftentimes feel choked out by all the distractions in the world.

Making a special effort to **monitor your feelings and emotions** and recognizing that you need help is a useful tool for the **backpack**. Find someone who can encourage you and help you to get back up and back on track. Remember, I mentioned earlier a useful tool for the backpack is scissors or a sharp tool to cut through the obstacles of your destination. This is useful for cutting out and eliminating the weeds in your life, especially when the landslides come.

When leading the college, I had to anticipate problems before they hit. While undergoing reaccreditation, we had to select a project that would move the college forward. Our project developed into a problem-solving model that we shared with all students to assist them with critical thinking and being able to solve problems. You can insert any problem in the exercise. I share this tool below:

EXERCISE (PROBLEM-SOLVING)

1. DEFINE: Identify and define the problem.

2. DESIGN: Analyze strategies/approaches for solving the problem.

3. SOLUTIONS: Propose potential solutions to the problem.

4. SELECTION: Select the best solution

5. ACTION PLAN: Develop a plan to resolve the problem.

6. EVALUATION: Evaluate the solution and implementation.

As an administrator, I found myself in the weeds quite often. This meant jumping in and doing things for people who should be doing things for themselves. Sometimes, you must know when to get out of the way. If we need to pull ourselves up by our bootstraps, we can have support, but really need to learn the value of the lesson by doing this on our own.

If you enable people's unproductive behaviors and take over for them, it can lead to burnout for you and rob others of the opportunity to gain experience in a new skill. Just like plants, you must fertilize when they have been in the ground for a long time.

BACKPACK TOOLS FROM CHAPTER 8

EMPATHY

SYMPATHY

COMPASSION

ACCEPTANCE

UNDERSTANDING

MONITOR YOUR FEELINGS/EMOTIONS

We must have a shot in the arm to boost our morale and get us going just like plants. Our plants need cultivating, watering, and lots of sunshine. If no plants are growing, it might be because there **ain't no sunshine**.

CHAPTER 9
Ain't No Sunshine

Oftentimes, when there is no sunshine, you might not feel like you have had a pick-me-up. This book would not be complete without the inclusion of the song "Ain't No Sunshine." Bill Withers was inspired by the film *Days of Wine and Roses* (1962) to write the song. The movie was about two alcoholics who were alternately weak and strong.

According to Withers, "Sometimes you miss things that weren't particularly good for you." The song was originally released as the backside to "Harlem," however, after DJs played the song as a single, it became a huge hit. It was released as a single in 1971 and peaked at number six on the Rhythm and Blues chart and at number three on the Billboard Hot 100 chart. There are many implications in this song that are a fit for acquiring tools for your backpack.

When it is dark and dreary in life, a pick-me-up is needed. I urge you to listen to this song and let the words speak to you. If you are a young person or elderly, this has implications for **YOU!** Do you ever remember a time in your life when you felt really low, really down, regardless of the reason? Perhaps you had a special person, a friend, a parent, a sibling, or someone you could tell your innermost secrets. This particular day, you were low as a snake and just needed to feel comfort from your special person, but unfortunately, he/she was not there for you. Maybe he/she was out of town, working, or just not there. It is especially difficult if that special someone is gone for a long time.

I remember a time in my young life when I was trying out for cheerleading in a new school. I practiced and practiced; however, I just could not get the routine down to make me stand out. As I competed along with others, I kept thinking about how good they were. I did not make the squad; however, my best friend did. I was devastated.

Upon hearing the news that I did not make it, I needed my special someone to rescue me from my dark, desolate feelings of worthlessness. My person was not around at the time, and I felt all alone. What I discovered at an early age was that, if you begin to have a pity party with yourself, it opens the door for other bad thoughts to enter. You begin to believe the negative thoughts.

I began to wonder what was wrong with me. Why was I not any good? Why was I not as talented as others? You see, negative breeds negative. If my special person had been there at that specific time, I would have shared these thoughts. Everything happens for a reason, and one of the best things that ever happened to me was NOT making the squad.

My special person did show up by the end of the day and reassured me that I did have skills and talents and to keep my head up and keep moving forward. I ended up trying out for the drill team, and not only did I make the squad, but also elevated very quickly to become a leader in the squad. I thoroughly enjoyed my years of dancing in the drill team and made lifelong friends. You never know the end result.

Everyone needs a special person in their life. Someone who (for lack of a better word) "lies" and insists that you are the prettiest in the class or the most talented on the team. We rely on these special people, and we need them desperately in our lives when there ain't no sunshine.

Backpack essential: a special person. What is desperately needed for your **backpack** is the realization that the **destination** is not what is important, but the **journey** along the way and how we manage the journey. I have learned more over my 60-plus years from the times that I have failed than those in which I have succeeded.

Sharing these times with your special person just makes it better. It allows the ownership to be shared, which lightens your load and picks you up.

The lyrics in this song remind me of the importance of animals in our lives. People who don't have a special person can have an animal–a cat, dog, horse, etc. There's no entity that loves you unconditionally as much as an animal. I could have the worst day ever at work and come home feeling low, and my dog would run out to greet me and be so excited to see me. They just love you no matter what. An **animal** can be one of the essentials for your **backpack**, especially in the tough times, and when there is no sunshine in your life.

"Ain't No Sunshine" reminds me of a song my mother used to sing to me, my grandmother used to sing to her, and my great-grandmother used to sing to my grandmother. I, too, have sung this song to my kids and grandkids. My children tell me that it is a morbid song; however, it shows that you are never alone when you are with animals. Even animals can bring you comfort. It is called "Old Shep." Composed by Red Foley and lyrics by Arthur Willis, the song was released in 1935 and was sung by Elvis Presley.

The song exemplifies the companionship between a boy and his dog and the fun times they have had growing up together. The boy ends up almost drowning in a swimming hole, and the dog jumps in and rescues the boy. The boy eventually has to put the old dog down. Although the song is sad, it emphasizes the importance and role that animals can play in our lives.

Think back to the first chapters in this book. Growing up, throughout the rough patches of my adolescence, my piano was my go-to. If I didn't have anyone to share my secrets, the tough times, or there was not any sunshine, I could go play on the ol' piano and feel better. So, inanimate objects, as well as animals, can be your special "pick-me-up" instead of a person.

I am reminded that as an adult working at the college how oftentimes my boss would have to go out of town. Now, you would think when the cat is away, the mice would play; however, it was a different case with me. It never failed when my boss was out of town there was always some kind of crisis or big issue that would happen, and I would have to make an important decision.

In the early days, there were no cell phones, so you could not just pick up the phone and call your boss whenever you wanted. On one of those occasions, serving in a supervisory position, I had a pretty big issue arise. I did not want to disturb my supervisor; therefore, I came up with a resolution to the problem at hand. It was not the perfect solution; however, it was one that was economical and one we could live with until the boss got back to town. When the boss got back and found out what I had done, would it appear the decision I made to fix the problem was incorrect? Worse, would I be blamed for letting the problem happen in the first place?

This self-doubt and worry were a blow to my ego, my intelligence, and my inner being. I needed my special person at this time, and my person was there for me. I felt so much better sharing how I felt. You see, when you share it, magic happens. Someone else takes ownership and there is power in numbers. Two is better than one when you are down. Upon the return of my boss, and once I explained the situation and reasoning behind my decision, my boss congratulated me on making a cost-effective decision.

My husband used to have to go out of town on business on occasion. There was always something coming up with our kids when he was away. Even though I could call him at the hotel, our house was not the same when he was gone.

Now, let us talk about darkness. The song implies darkness as a dreadful thing. You cannot see very well in the dark, which leads to accidents and all types of trouble. Light brings about clarity. My mom used to tell me, "Things will look better in the morning." There is truth to this statement. Whenever I've had something eating at me or issues, it always seemed better in the morning. Magically, I seem to have more clarity.

That is what light does; we can see better. Light from the sun provides warmth, which makes us feel better. It helps us to see, have clarity, and picks us up. When it's dark, we cannot see, we become fearful, and our imagination runs wild. Psychologists tell us light can improve our mood and stabilize our circadian rhythms, which helps us get more sleep. Light can decrease depression and mood.

I believe that light comes from people, too. Our special person brings light to us just at the right time when we need it the most. **Backpack tool: Go outside and get in the sunshine.** Even though there "ain't no sunshine when she's gone," there are things you can do in preparation for "when she comes back." Do something for someone else to help your mood until your person returns. If there ain't no sunshine and you have to stay indoors, there are things you can do to pick yourself up. For example, Jordan Upmails (1986), American Kennel Club recommends fun games to play with your dog.

EXERCISE (INDOOR ACTIVITIES WITH DOG)

1. Hidden Treasure. Arrange a few small boxes upside down throughout the house. Place a prize (treat) under one. When your dog finds the treat, congratulate and reward.

2. Hide and Seek–hide a treat under a chair.

3. Obedience Training–Have your dog retrieve obstacles and bring them back to you.

4. Obstacle Course–Set up boxes and get the dog to jump over the boxes.

5. Play Wild–Sits. Get your dog riled up and excited while on a leash, and then quickly ask him/her to sit.

6. Training Platform & Agility System–Configure a platform for your dog to sit on.

7. Cardio Twist–Set up poles or chairs in your house and have a dog weave in and out.

When I was teaching psychology at the college, one of my favorite exercises was to give my students "strengths test." I used CliftonStrengths Online Talent Assessment (1999). The students would take an assessment, and the results would give them their top five strengths. Knowing your strengths is important in helping you to stay positive when there ain't no sunshine.

My top five strengths were: achiever, communicator,

positivity, maximizer, and includer. An example of how I used my strengths as an includer was hosting events or parties at my house and ensuring everyone felt included by introducing them, asking them to help in the kitchen, and getting them involved in the discussions.

EXERCISE (STRENGTHS FINDER)

(A small fee might be required to access a code to take the CliftonStrengths Online Talent Assessment (1999) gallup.com/cliftonstrengths/en/strengthsfinder.aspx)

BACKPACK TOOLS FROM CHAPTER 9

SPECIAL PERSON

FOCUS ON THE JOURNEY NOT THE DESTINATION

MANAGE YOUR JOURNEY

ANIMALS

GO OUT INTO THE SUNSHINE

Even though there "Ain't no sunshine when she's gone," there are things you can do in preparation for "when she comes back." Knowing and emphasizing your strengths will help you with days of no sunshine. Do not let your imagination run away from you. Focus on the positive. Better days will return, and when there is sunshine, *I can see clearly*.

CHAPTER 10

I Can See Clearly Now

When you have experienced being picked up, an uplift if you will, you just seem to see more clearly. Unlike "Ain't No Sunshine," "I Can See Clearly Now" is an upbeat song emphasizing good things to happen and a bright sunshiny day. It was written and recorded by American singer Johnny Nash and released in the U.S. and UK in 1972, reaching number one on the US Billboard Hot 100. It also reached number one in Canada and South Africa, probably due to its positivity. You will enjoy listening to the lyrics of this song, especially when you feel you need a pick-me-up.

Individuals of any age need to be able to have vision and to see clearly. What is your vision? Do you know? Where are you heading? What is your purpose or mission for your life? Everyone needs to ponder their purpose. It's your blueprint. It tells you where you are headed just like the GPS/map and compass. It tells your story. You need to be able to see clearly to know where you are heading.

This is why a GPS/map and compass are good tools for the backpack. Your vision tells you where you choose to spend your time, money, and energy. It's where your heart lies. It is where your passions emerge, and your inspirations and motivations slip out. It will be your guiding light. It will dictate your priorities in your daily to-do list and how you choose to spend your time. To be able to see clearly is the heart of who we are.

We all have a purpose. We are not here at this time and at this place by accident. Your values and morals help shape who you will become. If you can see clearly, you can see your goals and where you are heading. Goals are like the end of the goalpost in football. You must get across it. Goals come from your values and vision/purpose. This is the result you want to achieve.

Every leader, college president, or CEO of an organization needs to have a vision. If you have people who are following you, they deserve to know where you are leading them in order to see clearly. Now, the important thing to know about vision is that you cannot keep it to yourself. If you are a leader, then you have followers. It is important to communicate your vision to your followers for them to (a) know where the institution/organization is going, and (b) in order for the employees to follow you, and (c) in order for them to see clearly.

Upon being appointed the 10th president of a community college, one of my first duties on the job was to communicate my vision to my administrators, faculty, staff, and students. I had a quite simple vision in order that my followers could understand and one that would help them see more clearly the path we were headed:

- Develop the college to be the college of choice

- Showcase the college to be an innovative institution of teaching and learning

- Promote student success

For you to clearly see my vision, I will explain. To be the college of choice meant that everything we did, we did for the students. Even though we did not have the most money or the best facilities, we put all our energies into ensuring that our students got the absolute best experience and personal attention they could possibly get.

What does it mean to showcase something? To tell our story, and to tell it well. This meant telling everyone about the many talented and credentialed faculty who worked at the college and showcasing their achievements.

Lastly, promoting student success was the most important concept of my vision. This meant to showcase and present all the great achievements of our students. Amazingly simple vision. The most difficult part of getting your followers to buy into your vision is helping them to understand it so they can see clearly. This is done by demonstrating repeatedly how you are accomplishing your vision.

Teachers, friends, and parents all help you to see more clearly and stay on task. My students used to tell me that they were not good at math or writing or playing sports. I used to tell them that everyone is a "10" at something. Not all people can grow to be a "10" in a specific skill, but everyone can be a "10" in attitude, desire, discipline, or perseverance.

For example, no matter how hard I have tried to excel at mathematics, I have never really excelled at this subject. However, through demanding work and studying, I found a way to pass. I had to understand the concepts, and once I could see them clearly, I could make it through. This song implies there will be problems and obstacles along the way. If you are seeing clearly, you will recognize the obstacles. Give them a name and take ownership of them. You can bypass them or hit them head-on if you know they are coming. Remember too, the scissors in the backpack to cut through the obstacles.

Tools for the backpack to continue to see clearly toward your goals:

A. **Plan your attack and attack your plan.** Everyone needs a goal, no matter your age. Hit it head-on and keep moving forward. Make a plan, follow your plan, and review your plan frequently. Identify unproductive time. Keep developing yourself and your plan. Find your niche and make yourself relevant.

B. **Do not overcommit.** One of the obstacles that get in the way is that we overcommit. We cannot say no. When asked to do something, we do it because we do not want to let others down. I have a challenging time with this. You cannot be your best if you do not have time for you. You must stay on track to get where you are going.

C. **Be flexible.** We are in a world where things go wrong every day. We must adjust, rethink, and start over several times a day to get back on track. It's okay and you have to be okay with this.

D. It is important to **reflect on how you got as far as you have.** Remember your sacrifices, remember the journey, share your journey so others can learn from your story. Friends, colleagues, and younger people are watching you and are following you. Be a good example because there just might be an influence you have on someone else.

EXERCISE (VISION)

1. Visualize where you want to be in five years. Think about the traits that you will need to attain your goal.

2. Visualize what you will look like in five years. Example: You want to be a nurse in five years.

3. Set measurable goals in writing, e.g., what do you need to accomplish in six months, one year, and three years to achieve your goals. Spell out the results you expect to achieve and how long it will take you.

4. Develop an action plan. How will you make this happen?

5. Get a picture of what you will look like in five years (upon accomplishing your goal) and place it on your refrigerator, where you will see it every day as a reminder of where you are headed.

6. Share your vision with a trusted friend or family member, who will hold you accountable.

BACKPACK TOOLS FROM CHAPTER 10

PLAN YOUR ATTACK/ATTACK YOUR PLAN

DO NOT OVERCOMMIT

BE FLEXIBLE

REFLECTION ON HOW FAR YOU HAVE COME

The exercise above will help you see clearly where you are heading. What is blinding you? What is keeping you from the person you were meant to be? What is keeping you from enjoying life and being where you want to be? What is keeping you from seeing clearly? Oftentimes, we simply need to slow down, get off the roller coaster, and ***sit on the dock of the bay***.

CHAPTER 11

Sittin' on the Dock of the Bay

Oh, how I love the song "Sittin' on the Dock of the Bay." It is my go-to song. Never have I ever felt more relaxed and picked up than enjoying nature, gazing out onto the water, and wasting time. Not only do I like the words in this song, but I also love the rhythm and beat.

Co-written by soul singer Otis Redding and guitarist Steve Cropper, it was recorded twice by Redding in 1967, including once just three days before his death in a plane crash in December 1967. The song was released on StaxRecord's Volt label in 1968, becoming the first-ever posthumous single to top the charts in the U.S. Redding wrote the lyrics to the song while sitting on a rented houseboat in Sausalito, California.

So, why do I like this song? First, I love the water. I have lived on a lake for over half of my life. There is just something relaxing and soothing about water. With the hustle and bustle of life, it is so calming to just sit and look at the water and watch the boats go by.

What is appealing about this song is that we all need a day to "do nothing but waste time." Why? To **reflect** and **rejuvenate** ourselves—good tools for the **backpack**. We are all in need of getting off the roller coaster for a period and being still. Not only are there health benefits to this, but also, it gives you time to think and reflect.

As I climbed the administrative ladder, having a day to unwind and do nothing became increasingly important to me. A necessity for the backpack, no matter your age. In the busy world we live in, with everything under the sun demanding our time, this is so important. You see, we are all on a roller-coaster. We get on, and it's all over the place, and although we do jump off on occasion, we jump back on. Having digital and social media at our fingertips 24 hours a day, how often do you truly unplug? Especially if you have children and a family, you work and engage in so many things and sometimes don't realize that time is passing you by.

To be the absolute best president I could be, I had to totally unwind at least once per week. Even mundane and petty things vied for my time. After the Christmas holidays and going into the new year, I always made a resolution to take one day per week to waste time and do nothing. I realized that I could not be my best as a president, a parent, a sibling, or a friend if I wasn't rested. This meant that I would have to prioritize my time and make time for resting. This meant totally unplugged from television, decisions at work, and, most importantly, the phone.

When was the last time you spent wasting time and doing nothing? I believe we have to learn what I call the "art of priority." To be totally in on the art of priority requires self-reflection about the things that are important to you and the things that matter to you. Have you unplugged enough lately to even know what is truly the most important thing to you? For me, people matter, which means I want to spend some focused time and energy building new relationships and fostering the relationships that I've already made. To be the best to others, you must work at it. It takes effort and sacrifice and requires self-discipline.

Just think about it. How sad is it that we must be "self-disciplined" to just sit on the dock of the bay wasting time? My issue was when I did unplug, I felt guilty that I was not working and was just wasting time. What I have found is that you can easily spend a lot of your time each day on things that give you absolutely NO return.

Here is a question to ponder if you find yourself in a situation where you are spending too much of your day being busy. Do I spend time during each day doing the things that are important to me and that really matter? Think about this question. We allow trivial, petty, and negative situations oftentimes to creep into our day, causing it to end up unproductive. One way to get around this is to make a list of the things you want to accomplish. At the end of the day, place a checkmark beside the ones that you accomplished. You will find that you spend some time on things that really do not matter.

Cutting the time you spend on the mundane allows more time for the important things. A technique that I frequently shared with my students that I suggest you try is called *The Pickle Jar Theory of Time Management* developed by Jeremy Wright (2002). This helped me to remember the important things that really matter.

I suggest trying this exercise at the end of this chapter. I modified the version to include golf balls. There are so many things that vie for our time daily. We celebrate so many freedoms in the United States, and one of those freedoms is the individual free will to choose what we do with our time.

When I was teaching, my students continually complained that they did not have time to do their assignments. Upon getting frustrated with this comment, I decided to give them an assignment from social psychologist Fritz Heider, developed in 1946. Dr. Heider developed a balance theory using a triangle to explain patterns of interpersonal relations; however, it can be applied to almost anything, e.g., attitudes, time, ideas, etc. I modified the original version for my students to give them an opportunity to check in on how balanced their lives were. My version went like this:

I asked the students to reflect on how much time they spent on three things: (a) school, (b) recreation, and (c) relationships. Now, we all know a triangle is a three-sided figure with sides. I asked the students to draw the first side of a triangle that represented how much time they think they spend on their schoolwork (in class, homework, etc.). Second, they drew another side of the triangle representing how much time they thought they spent on recreation (sports, T.V., games, etc.) Finally, I asked them to draw the final side of the triangle representing how much time they thought they spent on relationships (family, friends, significant other).

They were then asked to hold up their triangles and compare them to an actual three-sided triangle of equal sides. I never remember seeing a student's triangle resemble a true equilateral triangle. When you feel your life is out of balance, try this exercise. It is eye-opening to visually see where you are choosing to spend your time. **Balance theory exercise** is a useful tool for your **backpack**.

We must allow balance in our lives for health, relationships, rest, work, etc. If you are spending too much time on any one thing, the other things that are important get the short end of the stick.

You might have heard the cliché, "Take one day at a time." I take it a step further. My cliché is, "Take one minute at a time." In other words, where my attention is currently focused, I try to give it 100 percent of my attention while blocking out everything else.

EXERCISE (GOLF BALLS-PEBBLES-SAND)

First, you will need some supplies: a large clear jar, a box of golf balls, a box of sand, a box of pebbles, and two cups of coffee. The exercise goes like this:

1. Fill a large clear jar with all the golf balls that you can place in it. Ask yourself, *Is the jar full?* The answer is, "No."

2. Put a box of small pebbles in the jar. Now ask yourself, *Is the jar full yet?* Answer, "No."

3. Next, put a box of sand in the jar. *Is the jar full?* The answer is still "No."

4. Last, put two cups of coffee in the jar. *Is the jar full yet?* Answer, "Yes!"

Now, the secret to the story is that the jar represents your life. The golf balls are the important things in your life: faith, family, children, health, friends—things that if everything were lost and only they remained, your life would still be full.

The pebbles are the other things that matter…just not as important, such as job, house, and car. The sand is everything else…the small stuff. Things that we worry about but do not make a difference, e.g., housekeeping, washing clothes, going to meetings, etc.

What would happen if you were to put the sand in the jar first? There would be no room for the pebbles or the golf balls. By putting in the big, chunky things first and then letting the smaller things fill the spaces around it, we can fit more into the jar than if we tried to put things in as layers: first the sand, then the pebbles, then the golf balls. If you spend all your time and energy on the small stuff, that really doesn't matter, you'll never have room for the things that are important—people, faith, children, family.

This lesson exemplifies that you should pay attention to things that really matter to you. You know what they are. There is always time to clean, fix things, etc. If you set your priorities each day, placing emphasis on the things that matter, everything seems to fall into place. Now, you might be wondering where the coffee fits into the picture. No matter how full your life might seem, there is always room for a couple of cups of coffee with a friend while sittin' on the dock of the bay, wastin' time. Take care of the golf balls because the rest is just sand.

BACKPACK TOOLS FROM CHAPTER 11

FIND TIME TO WASTE SOME TIME

REFLECTION

REJUVENATION

BALANCE THEORY EXERCISE

GAZE UPON THE WATER

Where will you place sittin' on the dock on your priority list? When have you simply **wasted time**? Put it in your **backpack**! For me, I make time to sit and **look at the water**, another useful tool for the **backpack**. Maybe that is why I moved to a lake. It clears my head, helps me to prioritize, and reassures me of a *promise* of good things to come…

CHAPTER 12
Hymn of Promise

I purposefully left the song "Hymn of Promise" for the latter part of the book as it speaks volumes about who I am. It gives me the pick-me-up that I need. People sense and feel differently when the flowers start blooming and the birds and bees start singing. Every spring, I feel a sense of being picked up due to the rebirth and renewal of God's spring bouquet because of its significance to life, death, grief, seasons, music, etc.

The **"Hymn of Promise"** was written in 1934 as an anthem by Natalie Sleeth. It was written as a reawakening of the world as happens every spring; however, it ended up being a request by her husband, who had a terminal illness, to be played at his funeral.

This song has been played numerous times at funerals and in church worship services. I recommend you spend some time listening to the lyrics and discover what they mean to you. This is definitely a song about hope. We all need hope. **Hope** deserves to be in your **backpack**. We all need to have something to look forward to.

We all need to know and expect that things will keep changing for the better. The only thing that is constant about change is change. We know that if you plant a bulb and it gets water and light, it will become a flower. However, it does not end there. You must continue watering, fertilizing, and giving the bulb light. The good news is that a bulb will come back next year.

Apples come from seeds. Butterflies come from cocoons. Things may start from the smallest of things but will become something. Listen up! This is for **YOU!** You might not feel worthy nor good enough. You might not feel talented nor pretty, nor fast or strong, BUT you have skills and abilities that no one else has. You are your own unique person. You are a ten at something! You must discover what the ten is and then spend time perfecting and using your ten. The seasons of life show us that after the long, snowy days of winter, flowers bloom, birds begin to chirp, and spring is around the corner. There is predictability in seasons, and we see the signs by the position of the sun and moon and the falling and renewal of leaves on the trees.

Songs don't just create themselves. People put words together to make a song and then a melody to fit. You have creativity unlike any other. You might not know what it is yet but keep looking. What gives you pleasure, what makes you happy, what do you like spending your time on?

When I was serving as a counselor, I spent many years helping students discover what to major in during their college years. I would give them a variety of personality and aptitude tests to help them see where their interests lie. To no avail, upon receiving their results, there were always a few students who would get upset because they did not agree with the results. I would tell them the assessments were simply a tool to assist them with information to help with their decision-making process. I would tell them to do things that bring them joy and happiness and not to select a career just because of the money they can make.

Oftentimes, people end up in careers as a process of

elimination. You try something and if you are not happy, you move on to something else and eventually land in a field that makes you happy. Tools, such as **personality** and **aptitude assessments**, help us with decision-making for the future and are great tools for your **backpack**.

"Hymn of Promise" indicates that the future is a mystery. We don't know what the future holds, and it is yet to be revealed; however, we have faith that good will come, and we will have something to contribute. I have recently ended a 41-year career in higher education, and although I miss my colleagues and students, it was time to end. Is it scary? Yes. Do I know what the future holds for me? No. What I do know is that I am sitting down drafting a book for YOU!

I have never done this before. There is a chance that it will not get published. There is a chance no one will purchase the book if it is published. What I do know is that I had a calling to get beyond myself and try to help others who might have experienced some of the things I have experienced and can learn from me. That is why I am sharing the contents of my backpack.

When anticipating things to come and questioning my purpose in life, I oftentimes reflect on a sign that my husband gave me when we married. The sign reads as follows: "Think about the past, look to the future, but live now." He bought me this sign so I could remember to live "now." As I embarked on a new journey, I began by looking back at the good memories I shared with others, whether they were ones of laughter, unique events, or ones not so good. It is healthy to remember the relationships you have encountered along the way. It is okay to remember the painful times. While you cannot change these nor go back, you can learn from previous mistakes and find ways to move forward.

I also looked to the future in anticipation and where I was

headed. This was dangerous for me because I am a planner and was always planning out everything before it happened. However, as my husband so eloquently reiterated, if I spend so much time looking back or looking ahead, I might miss and enjoy the journey in front of me. You can learn from me. That's why I am sharing the contents of my backpack.

Although there is uncertainty when looking at the future, there are steps that we can take to help us prepare for the future. One of those steps is to take a hard look at ourselves. We play multiple roles in our lives, and these roles define who we are and how we spend our time. These roles change with time, and our priorities change as we age. It is important to take a look at the roles that we play. The exercise below can help you get started on a good reflection of yourself.

EXERCISE (WHO AM I?)

1. Write down at least eight to ten roles that you currently play. Example: mother/father, artist, caregiver, etc.

2. Arrange these roles from what you think are the most important to the least important.

3. Look at the least important role that you listed. Could you live without serving in that role? Ask this question about the other roles you listed.

4. Take away your most key role that you listed. What does that feel like if you were not in that role?

5. Envision your future. Make a list of what roles you feel you will have in the future. Do you see your roles changing in the future? What roles do you believe will be the hardest to balance in the future? What roles will make your life complete?

6. Are you happy with the roles that you currently play? Is there anything that would make them better?

This exercise makes you think about the many roles you play and those roles that you feel are necessary to give you hope for the future.

BACKPACK TOOLS FROM CHAPTER 12

HOPE

PERSONALITY/APTITUDE ASSESSMENTS

We all need to believe in something. For me, relationships, contributing, and getting beyond myself to help others allow me to **turn the page**.

Turn the Page

Just simply by turning the page, you could possibly be picked up! I felt a need to include the song "Turn the Page" because it has implications for all of us, and there are lessons to be learned from the words. The lyrics remind me that life is a struggle and the only one in control of how you feel and who you are is **YOU**. We must reach a point to pick our own selves up when we are down.

We are in control of our own destinies. This song was originally recorded by Bob Seger in 1971 and released on his "Back in 72" album in 1973. The song has always been extremely popular and received a lot of airplay on classic rock stations. The story in this song is about the emotional and social difficulties of a rock musician's life on the road. Although I am not a rock musician, I know what it feels like to be on the road or roller coaster for extended periods of time and just need to get off.

This song truly resonates with me because my life has been a series of difficulties regardless of whether I was driving, riding, or sitting at home. We all have experienced lengthy periods of what I call drought, where we are uninspired, and we question why we keep doing the same thing over and over and expect different results. We all get in a funk at times and just cannot seem to get out of it. When we do, life might seem hopeless, uncertain, and unfulfilling. Can you relate?

I had an acquaintance in another life who was a truck driver. He invited me to go on the road with him, which consisted of driving across Texas from El Paso to Marshall. I cannot imagine doing that every day all day. This was a time before smartphones. The only thing you have to do is think. It was difficult for someone like me, who is highly active and likes to move around a lot. These "funk" times can be termed "depression," "worthlessness," and many other terms. Regardless, you don't feel much like doing anything. Can you relate to a time in your life when you felt this way?

When teaching psychology, my students used to ask me what it was like to have major depression. I told them I had not ever experienced it; however, it was probably like being in a hole. When one thing is going well in your life and everything else is bad, you can still function and keep going. When you cannot find anything going well in your life, you just feel hopeless and feel like you are in a hole and you can't get out.

I've been on the road for long stretches of time and physically and mentally felt worn out at the end of the day. I couldn't wait to get out of the car, and I dreaded getting back in. We all have experienced long stretches in our lives, where we felt down and unworthy, where it seems like one day was just like the next one, and they all run together.

Can you relate to this musician being on the road all the time trying to make it? Every gig played is like the last. It is a hard life, I imagine, and we all might be able to relate. To someone on a career path like this, every day is more of the same. It's like turning the page and finding the same ol' thing.

What can you do? It is up to you to turn the page to a new chapter, to something new and different. When you wake up every day, you have a choice. You can be down, or you can have gratitude for just waking up and being given the opportunity for another day. I call it having an attitude of gratitude.

Attitude is critical in determining what type of day we will experience. Attitude applies to almost any situation. I am amazed no matter how much you do for people; you will always find someone who is ungrateful and takes for granted the help you have given. *Webster's Dictionary* defines "gratitude" as the quality of being thankful; readiness to show appreciation for and to return kindness. We have the opportunity to be thankful and show appreciation for freedom like no other country. Many of us have the blessings of having a consistent place to eat, sleep, work, and play. We have the opportunity to worship, the opportunity of free speech, and the opportunity to work. Where is gratitude?

Have you ever noticed how people come together in a tragedy or a crisis? Think about the World Trade Center attack on 9/11 and how law enforcement, firefighters, police officers, first responders, and citizens came together to help. When the pandemic hit a couple of years ago, did you notice how the government, medical professionals, and responders came together in unity to assist those in need? Can't we do the same for individuals in crisis? Where is the civility, compassion, and empathy for others? I believe it starts with us and reaching out to those in need.

I believe having an **attitude of gratitude** is worthy of your **backpack**. It is a learned behavior. When we are children, we observe it and watch it in those around us. We bring these early observations that we learned into adulthood with us. Is it too late to develop an attitude of gratitude? My answer is no. As mentioned earlier, in the fitness world, you cannot practice lifting weights one time and expect to develop muscles. Similarly, you must monitor your attitude and practice over and over having an attitude of gratitude.

Attitude is a choice. Can you think of a person in your life who makes you feel good to be around? Although your paths might not cross frequently, when they do, you always come away blessed. Have you ever met anyone who made you feel honored and blessed to be around? Some people just have the uncanny ability to make you feel better leaving than when you arrived.

All through my career, there were times that I questioned my purpose, and I asked myself if I should change something to make life more meaningful. When I felt this way, I found time during the evening to do some journaling. This allowed me to get my thoughts down on paper about how I was feeling at the time. The significance of journaling is to go back several days later and read what you wrote. You might find that what you wrote of concern was no longer applicable. **Journaling** is a great tool for the **backpack** only if you remember to go back later and read what you wrote.

A great exercise that helped me focus on my current behavior and determine if changes were needed was to complete a behavior modification plan. Psychology offers many behavior modification plans; however, I developed my own simplistic model to satisfy my own needs. This exercise helped me to get back on track after what I felt were long, mundane times in my life.

EXERCISE (BEHAVIOR MODIFICATION)

1. Identify a specific behavior that you would like to change or improve in yourself. The behavior needs to be one that is observable.

2. Develop a few steps or goals to either decrease or increase the behavior you want changed.

3. Reward or treat yourself every time you catch yourself performing the correct behavior. If you catch yourself performing incorrect behaviors, take away an activity or privilege.

4. Keep a log of your performance.

5. Share your results with a friend or family member.

BACKPACK TOOLS FROM CHAPTER 13

ATTITUDE OF GRATITUDE

JOURNALING

When you turn the next page in your own journey, where will you find yourselves? Will you be a risk taker and take the next leap? Will you go on a totally new journey? Perhaps a journey that you have never been on before?

You only have one shot at life, maybe it is time to begin anew. Remember, what I intend to be begins with me. This can even be done while you are riding for sixteen hours and there is nothing else to do. This is **YOUR** life and **YOUR** time. You only get one shot at this world. This is **YOUR** *story* to tell...

CHAPTER 14

The Story

In completing this book, there is but one song to end with. It's one of my favorites. **"The Story"** is a song released as a single by American folk-rock singer, Brandi Carlile, written by Phil Hanseroth, from her 2007 album, The Story. This song was also featured in the television show, *Grey's Anatomy*, 2007, and is on *Grey's Anatomy Soundtrack* album three.

This song is about all of us. You and me! As stated once again, we are in control of how we feel. We are in control of what kind of day we will have. We all have a choice in how we spend our time, our money, and our relationships. Bottom line: we have the ability to pick ourselves up anytime and anywhere.

Who doesn't like a delightful story? Why is it that we remember stories oftentimes more than a speech, a presentation, or a sermon? Stories have the uncanny ability to identify with us. They bring value to us.

Psychologists tell us that we are all born as a blank slate. In other words, we are born blank until life, people, friends, and parents imprint on us. Although we have certain biological traits we inherit from parents, our surroundings begin to imprint on us at an incredibly early age. Let me give you an example. We begin buying pink clothing and decorating baby girls' rooms in pink even before they are born, and blue for boys. We treat girls differently by telling them to be ladylike, not to be rough and tough. It is just the opposite with boys. We teach them to be tough and rough and not to cry. Kids begin to assimilate to their surroundings and begin taking on roles according to the expectations of those around them.

Fast forward, have you looked in the mirror lately? What do you see? When I was raising kids and working, I never really had a lot of time to reflect on who I am and what my life would represent. Now that my children are grown, and I've retired, I've had time to reflect on my next chapter. Looking into the mirror at my age, I see many more lines on my face than I used to. Instead of looking for the latest and greatest creams and products to erase these lines, I am embracing them. This song illustrates that lines represent the story of who we are and where we have been.

Psychologist Robert Sternberg's (1986) *Triangular Theory of Love* suggests there are three components of love: intimacy (closeness, sharing communication), passion (emotional aspect of love and to being united with one), and commitment (short-term affirmation and long-term commitment to maintain love.)

As I reflect on my career, I can honestly say that I subscribe to a triangular love for the field of education and my work as an administrator. Sternberg's **Theory of Love components, intimacy, passion, and commitment** are worthy of your **backpack**.

Through daily communication with colleagues, sharing of the good and tough times, and supporting those in our work family who went through grieving, I experienced what Sternberg referred to as intimacy. I definitely had a passion for the field of education. This was reflected in the many presentations given to parents, businesses, and organizations over the years. I truly felt united with my colleagues and students.

Lastly, and the one that I definitely feel I've achieved, is commitment. My short-term commitments evolved into long-term goals to maintain intimacy and passion and to keep moving forward. Commitment to me means "in it for the long haul." I guess you can say after 41 years, I was definitely in the business for the long haul. In a world of instant gratification, it is difficult to see people with stick-to-itiveness and being committed. Are you willing to withhold immediate gratification and pleasure for a deeper, richer purpose?

One of the things I am most proud of is growing up in a small town without much money. My brothers and I didn't know we didn't have money because we were rich with love from parents, grandparents, and friends. We did not have a lot of toys; however, we didn't need them. We used our imaginations and played outside in the trees and neighborhood. What this experience taught me now that I'm retired and don't have a regular job with a salary, is how to live on a shoestring. I know how to make food and money stretch.

This story, for which I am thankful, prepared me for my later years. Your stories of childhood will follow you into adulthood, some good and some not so good. What stories from your early childhood have shaped you as an adult?

Another story from childhood that had a profound influence on me was how hard I had to study to get good grades. High academic achievement did not come naturally to me. I had an attention span about like a remote control. My mind would race from one thing to the next. In school, when assigned to read, I found myself reading the same paragraph over and over and could not begin to tell you what it was about.

Somehow, as I aged, I learned techniques to help me stay more focused, such as getting in a quiet room free from distractions, studying for hours, having my mom question me about what I read, etc. These experiences taught me the art of perseverance. I had to dig and study harder than the average person to learn. As I enrolled in college and began to learn about myself, I realized that my learning style was one of being visual and kinesthetic.

In other words, I must see things and be interactive in the learning process to really get it. This really shaped who I was. It took me ten years to graduate from college with a bachelor's degree. Partly because I went back to school after having children and had to take one course at a time and drive seventy-five miles one way to college, all while working full time. I desperately wanted to go to graduate school; however, in those days, you had to pass the Grade Record Exam (GRE) and score high enough to get into college. Working on my bachelor's degree, I learned how to retain and make good grades, but test-taking was exceedingly difficult for me. I had a lot of anxiety about tests and always expected the worst.

Nonetheless, after deciding to get a graduate degree, I took the Graduate Record Exam five times. I always did well in the writing section but had difficulty with the math section. This experience made me feel like a failure in math and less than. Ever been there? Ever felt this way? I even went to a university and enrolled in a GRE prep course to no avail, and still didn't do well on the GRE math. I just totally gave up on the idea of going to graduate school, although I had a 3.5 GPA in undergraduate education.

A couple of years later, while working and raising kids, I received a letter from a university that I had previously applied. It announced I had been accepted into their graduate program. What the heck? Was this a mistake? I called them and they indicated my undergraduate GPA was good enough to get in on a probationary basis. Ever been on probation? It does not feel particularly good. Makes you feel less than. Guess what? I graduated with a Doctor of Education Degree with a 4.0.

The point of this "story" is that these experiences created a lot of lines on my face, but it tells of where I have been and how I got to where I am now. Had I not always had a tough time with school, I would not have known how to persevere. I learned a valuable lesson, which fits nicely in the **backpack**: when you fail, you **persevere, pull yourself up** by your bootstraps, and keep going.

These experiences helped me to become a good counselor and share my experiences with students at the college level, especially those who had test anxiety. They helped me to be a better administrator and sympathize with employees who were having difficulty. This is my story, and this is who I am. I am not ashamed of it. I learned from it. What does your story say about you? What have you learned from your experiences?

Something I learned in leadership when collaborating with teams was from John Maxwell's book, *Developing the Leader Within* (1993). Not all producers/performers in an organization are at the top of the team. According to Maxwell, 10% of producers in a department are considered top producers, 10% of the players are considered low performers, but 75% of workers who oftentimes produce are in the middle. These folks can be the backbone of an organization and need to be valued and encouraged. I fell in the middle of the road. Nothing has ever come easy for me, and I had to work to get where I am. What about you? Where do you land?

I believe this song tells us that our stories from various stages of development, ethnicities, races, and backgrounds don't mean anything if we don't tell them to someone. Our children and grandchildren need to hear our stories. This might just be our legacy that we leave them.

Upon becoming president of a college, I was asked to write

a monthly column for a local newspaper, which ended up being three local newspapers. Because I was so busy covering three campuses and going to college events, I had little time to write these articles.

My assistant always reminded me that the article was due the day before, and as usual, I ended up writing it at the last minute before the deadline. I prayed that the words would come, and God did not disappoint. I would think of a story about a student and begin to write.

There is a benefit to being in the education field, and especially teaching, in that you have a lot of student stories that you can tell. The times I found myself scurrying to get the article written, it was always easy for me to write about student experiences. Without any doubt, every time I drafted a story about a student, people in the community came up to me, thanking me for writing such a delightful story. Although I changed the names, the stories were all true. I even had individuals tell me that they were going to cancel their subscription to the newspaper but decided not to because they loved reading my stories.

We all have a story, and it needs to be told to someone.

Backpack resource: write down or tell your story and put it in your **backpack**. Pull it out on occasion and keep adding to it as you age. Your children, your grandchildren, and your friends will appreciate reading them one day. People really do not know what **YOU** have been through or what **YOU** are going through. You can tell them, but until they walk in your shoes, they really don't know how you feel. Many people over the years told me how "lucky" I was to be smart and have a respectable job. They did not know how hard it was for me to do well in school, retain information, and climb the ladder of success. I never told them the struggles I experienced being hyperactive. I never told them that I was always the average" student. *What are you hiding?* I'd ask myself.

My head was always a mess because it had a million and one things running through it every second, every minute of the day. It was always so hard for me to focus. I just learned tricks and techniques to help me focus. I did all of this without medication, too. I learned the art of perseverance.

"The Story" from this last chapter requires us to review where we have started on our life's journey and where we have ended up thus far. When my students used to fret that they didn't know what to major in or where they were heading, I would give them the reflection exercise below to help them see how far they had come in life. We all have highs and lows in our lives, but if we are moving forward, we are making progress.

EXERCISE (REFLECTION OF LIFE)

1. Develop a timeline of your life starting at whatever point fits your situation. You can start in elementary school, college, or later in life. You can do this by age, date, or year.

2. Look at your life and list the most memorable times you can remember in your life. These are times that you were the happiest. These are positive times in your life. Examples: graduation, birth of a child, promotion at work, etc.

3. Look at your life and list the most trying times of your life.

4. After the exercise, reflect on how far you have come in life, despite challenges. Have you learned any lessons from the trying times? Do you see any reoccurring patterns in your life?

5. End the exercise with comments about how far you have come in life.

6. List any goals for the future that you would like to begin to help you keep moving forward.

BACKPACK TOOLS FOR CHAPTER 14

STERNBERG'S THEORY OF LOVE (INTIMACY, PASSION, COMMITMENT)

PERSEVERANCE

PULL YOURSELF UP

WRITE DOWN YOUR STORY

TELL YOUR STORY TO SOMEONE

I believe that it's healthy to occasionally reflect on where we started on our journey and how far we've come despite the obstacles on our path. Although people really don't know who you are or what you've been through, it is important to **stay true to you**!

In with the New...
While Staying True to You

Question: How do you stay true to yourself while on your life's journey?

Answer: Carry a backpack that is filled with tools you've gathered along the way that are unique to YOU.

While on your journey, your backpack is essential to carry the things you need to get you through life. My story is nothing special. I was an average girl, growing up with little money but a lot of love, who had to work harder than the average person to get where I was going. I loved music, which became a significant part of my life and helped me cope with the tough times. I started out as a telephone operator at a community college and, after 41 years, retired as the president.

In this journey of mine, and now reflecting back, I can share that my intentions in life were to:

Give the world something

it did not know it was missing.

Be an agent of change.

Tell the world my own unique story.

Pick myself up.

As an educator, I wanted to lead and prepare students for entry into higher education and/or entry into the workforce. My overriding theme was one of student achievement, student engagement, and student success. When students succeeded, I succeeded. I wanted to provide excellence in education and quality education, and most importantly, I wanted to give students the tools they needed for their backpacks to survive and compete in a global and competitive society.

Just like me, **YOU**, no matter what age you are, need to find your niche. When the niche starts to change, after you have become comfortable in it, you will experience stress and insecurities. You will experience feelings of unworthiness… that you are not smart enough…nor good enough. But remember, you are a "10" at something. It might be attitude. Remember, this is your story. You must write your own. I think for me, my theme was "persistence."

Every product in America has too many choices. You are going to have to acquire skills to navigate through these vast amounts of choices you will have to make for your journey. The journey ahead will require you to live in a world of plenty and abundance. During the 20th century, the aspiration of most middle-class Americans was to own a home and car. Now, in the 21st century, two out of three Americans own the homes they live in and have at least two cars.

We have so much "stuff" that the self-storage business is a $17 billion annual industry. We spend more money on trash bags than ninety countries do on anything else.

How can **YOU** be equipped to live in a conceptual age

with the tools you need to be successful? Your backpack will need to contain tools to manage the detours, the barriers, the side roads, and the curves in the road, tailored for your own unique trip.

Have any of these pages spoken to **YOU**? Have you felt a pick-me-up? If so, get you a backpack and arm yourself with the tools you'll need no matter what age you are. So, where am I in all of this? After retiring, I made myself a promise to give myself one year to see what this retirement thing is all about. I must tell you that I have been blessed with an incredible year. I have been fortunate enough to do some traveling and see some places on my bucket list.

During this year, I have experienced the marriage of my son and the birth of my fourth grandchild. Lastly, I began drafting this book. God has truly blessed me this first year of retirement.

So, what is my next story?

I recognize that I'm going through what psychologist Erick Erikson explains so well as his stages of development, which you can find in any developmental psychology book. I taught about these stages for six years and certainly recognize that I am going through what is called "generativity versus stagnation." Simply put, upon retiring, I now have the time to discover my sense of purpose, as well as begin to give back to society. Erickson looks at this stage in life as one where conflict may occur. If people at this stage cannot find their sense of purpose nor have the desire to contribute and give back to society, they can experience what is called stagnation.

Well, believe me, I am anything but stagnant. Someone as hyper as me, who cannot sit still, coupled with my sense of wanting to be a helper, keeps me motivated and moving forward. I recognize that I am going through another phase of life, but for the first time, I am enjoying seeing various parts of the world. My day is made by a drop-in visit from my grandson, who wants to go look for dinosaur fossils at the lake.

I am enjoying keeping my hummingbirds fed and watching the males run off the females from the feeders. My crepe myrtles are blooming for the first time in June and definitely live up to their fire engine red name. I have been blessed to spend time with my 89-year-old mother and go to the farmers market, and oh, what joy it is when I get to spend time holding my three-month-old grandson and watching him go through his first stages of life. My life has a purpose for these important people who are in it.

My backpack is full, and I find that through retirement, I am having to reach down deep into the bottom of the pack to pull out tools I haven't used in a while. The essentials I carry in mine and pull out from time to time will be different for each of you according to your own story and your own destination.

Looking at life as if you are on a journey brings benefits such as satisfaction in realizing your accomplishments, helping others, and the hope of things to come at a time when people need to feel valued. It is important to reflect back to those individuals who said a kind word, a teacher who taught you more than a subject, or a counselor who held your hand along the way.

Remember to thank these people and to celebrate how far you have come. As you take off on a new journey, and believe me, you will, to new unchartered territory, you might have to discard your backpack for a new one. You may find just like people; your backpack may be tattered around the edges. The pockets may no longer zip to contain the essentials you need. Choose wisely in selecting a new one. You may need a larger backpack for the next journey to help you weave the many paths and turns that come along the way. When you feel you are nearing the end of a journey, take out the tools that helped you get where you were going and share them with others in need of light and direction.

I hope you will place emphasis on the tools you are placing in your backpack. You must not get caught up looking at your backpack as a bag of excuses but rather as a bag of opportunities. Just because you might be lacking a certain tool for your backpack does not mean you cannot go on the journey. It is important when the door of opportunity knocks, that you dig deep in the pack and pull out what you need.

Excuses run rampant in our society today and can be contagious because they require less of us. "I don't have time," "I am too tired," and "I don't know how" are the most popular excuses that you will hear. Throw your bag of excuses away, focus on your backpack essentials, and embark on your journey ahead.

Happy travels with your new tools for your backpack, and remember it is not the destination that is important, but how you manage the journey along the way…so, what is stopping you? Put the book down and begin looking for, finding, and placing your tools in your own **backpack**. Share your journey with others along the way. This is your own unique story. There is no better time to start your journey than NOW! See you on the trail… I hope you are glad you picked this up!!!!

Recap of My Song Playlist and Tools for the Backpack

Additional Tools
for Your Backpack

Making Sense of Things—As we see ever-changing social media, you are going to have to make intelligent interpretations and be able to provide insight to make effective decisions.

Social Intelligence—Relationships and connecting with others in a direct and meaningful way will be important.

Flexible Thinking—You'll have to problem solve and figure things outside of the box to produce solutions that people do not know they need.

Global Intentionality—We are globally connected by our smartphones, and the ability to operate in diverse cultures and global settings will help you stand out and get ahead.

Literacy with Social Media—New emerging social media platforms are constantly being developed. You'll have to know how to make connections across vast networks and platforms and stay on top of emerging technologies.

Management of Information—Think of all the many diverse types of shampoos on the market. One for sensitive hair, one for oily hair, one for dry hair, etc. You will need skills to be able to filter out what is important and right for you. Knowing how to make choices and filter through vast amounts of information will be important.

Decision Making—Make decisions on how to sift through the "abundance" to determine what is important and where you are headed.

Receptivity—Be receptive to opportunities to avoid drifting or wandering along the path.

Discovery of Self—Discover your own strengths that you'll need to open doors that you choose to knock on along the road and listen to your own voice.

Embracing Change—Embrace changing your destination, acquiring new tools, and developing the ones you already possess.

Recognition—Recognize that the more tools you have on your journey, the more doors that will be open to you.

Being Active—Get your hands dirty, fall on your face, and learn to get back up and go again. Take charge of your own destination.

Dr. B's Final Thoughts for the Trip

- Align YOUR values with time, what you enjoy, and your own interests.

- Visualize what success looks like on you.

- Educate and equip yourself for success.

- Empower yourself to reach into your own **backpack** for tools that you will need for your journey, pull them out, and actively use them.

- The greatest rewards in life will be in the journey, not the destination. Embrace change and difference and create something that others did not know they needed.

- Do not be afraid to pick yourself up.

GO AHEAD…PICK ME UP!

References

Arrien, Angeles (1991). Lessons from Geese. Organizational Development Network. Based On work from Milton Olsen. *Tools for Change.*

Austin, Daryl (2023) *Laughter is Really Contagious—and That's Good.* Retrieved June 5, 2024 from http://www.wahingtonpost.com/wellness/2023/01/15/laughting-is-contagious/

Brookfield, S. (n.d.) Creating critical classrooms. Retrieved from http://www.stephenbrookfield.com

Brown, M.N., & Meuti, M.D. (1999). Teaching how to teach critical thinking. *College Student Journal, 33*(2), 162-170.

Cheung, C., Rudowicz, E., Kwan, A. S., & Yue, X. (2002). Assessing university students' general and specific critical thinking. *College Student Journal,36*(4), 504-525. What is critical thinking? (2005). Retrieved from http://www.criticalthinking.com/company/articles/critical-thinking-definition.jsp

Eiseley, Loren C. (1969). The Starfish Thrower. *The Unexpected Universe.* San Francisco, California.

Ennis, R. (2002). A super streamlined conception of critical thinking. Retrieved from http://www.criticalthinking.com/company/articles/critical-thinking-definition.jsp

Erickson, Eric (2002). *Dictionary of the Social Sciences.* Oxford University Press. ISBN: 9780199891184.

Foley, Red (1935). *Old Shep*. American Record Corporation, Chicago, IL.

Fulghum, Robert (1986). Thoughts on Common Things. *All I Really Know, I Learned in Kindergarten. Uncommon Thoughts On Common Things*. Random House Publishing Inc. ISBN: 978-0-345-46639-6 New York: New York.

Gallup (1999). CliftonStrengths Assessment. Gallup. Retrieved June 30, 2024 from https://www.gallup.com/cliftonstrengths/en/home.aspx

Harlow, Harry (1958). Rhesus Monkeys Attachment. *Mastering the World of Psychology*. p. 268. Pearson Education, Inc. Upper River, N.J.

Heider, Fritz (1946). Attitudes and Cognitive Organization. *Journal of Psychology*, 21, 107-112.

Higgins, E. Tory; Roney, Christopher, J.R., Crowe, Ellen, & Hymes, Charles (1984). "Ideal Versus Ought Predictions for Approach and Avoidance Distinct Self-Regulatory Systems." *Journal of Personality and Social Psychology*. 66(2): 276-286.

Huitt, W. (1998). Critical thinking: An overview. *Educational Psychology Interactive*. Valdosta, GA: Valdosta State University. Retrieved from http://www.edpsycinteractive.org/topics/cogsys/critthnk.html

Landis, M., Swain, K., Friehe, M., & Coufal, K. (2007). Evaluating Critical Thinking in Class and Online: Comparison of the Newman Method and the Facione Rubric. *Communication Disorders Quarterly Spring 2007 28*: 135-143.

Mayo Clinic Staff (Sept. 22, 2023). *Stress Relief From Laughter? It's No Joke*. Minnesota. Retrieved 6/10/2024 from http://www.mayoclinic.org/healthy-lifestyle

Maxell, John (1993). *Developing the Leader Within You*. Harper Collins, Nashville, TN. ISBN: 9780718074081.

Merriam-Webster.com Dictionary, Merriam-Webster, https://www.merriam-webster.com/dictionary/community. Accessed 1 Jul. 2024.

Merriam-Webster.com Dictionary, Merriam-Webster, https://www.merriam-webster.com/dictionary/gratitude. Accessed 1 Jul. 2024.

Merriam-Webster.com Dictionary, Merriam-Webster, https://www.merriam-webster.com/dictionary/joy. Accessed 1 Jul. 2024.

Owen, Julie E.; Komives, Susan R.; Lucas, Nance; McMahon, Timothy R. (2007). *Exploring Leadership: For College Students Who Want to Make a Difference*, 2nd ed. John Wiley & Sons, Inc. San Francisco, CA.

Paul, R & Edler, L.(2009). Critical thinking development: A Stage theory. Retrieved from http://www.criticalthinking.org/page.cfm?PageID=483&CategoryID=68

Paul, R., Elder, L., & Bartell, T. (1997). *California teacher preparation for instruction in critical thinking: Research findings and policy recommendations.* Dillon Beach, CA: The Foundation for Critical Thinking.

Peterson, Jonathan (Oct. 6, 2014). What to Say Before Amen: An Interview With Max Lucado. Retrieved 6/1/2024 from a blog www.biblegateway.com

Piscitelli, S. (2008). *Study skills-Do I really need this stuff?* (2[nd]ed.). Upper Saddle River, NJ: Pearson Prentice Hall. Hill College 61.

Rath, Tom. 2007. *StrengthsFinder 2.0.* New York, NY: Gallup Press.

Reflective thinking: RT. (n.d.) Retrieved from http://www.higp.hawaii.edu/kaams/resource/reflection.htm

Ruggiero, V. (2009). *The art of thinking: A Guide to critical and creative thought.* New York: Longman.

Sternberg, Robert (1986). A Triangular Theory of Love. *Psychological Review*, 93(2), 119-135, Washington, D.C.

Theopedia. Retrieved 7/1/22/24 from www.theopedia. com › joy.

Upmails, Jordan (2022). *Fun Indoor Games to Play With Your Dog.* American Kennel Club. Retrieved 5/31/2024 from http://www.akc.org/expert-advice/Lifestyle/great-indoor-games-to-play-with-your-dog

Wright, Jeremy (2002). The Pickle Jar Theory. *A List Apart.* Retrieved 5/15/2024 from http://www.alistapart.com/article/pickle

About the Author

Dr. Pam Boehm grew up in Hubbard Texas. Upon graduating from high school, she obtained a secretarial certificate from Hill College and then moved to Irving Texas, where she was employed for three years working as a legal secretary for Mary Kay Cosmetics, Inc. With a desire to finish her education, she moved back to Hill County and enrolled at McLennan Community College and earned an Associate of Arts Degree. She was hired in July of 1978 at Hill College as a switchboard operator and then assistant to the Dean of Instruction. After ten years in this position, she quit to pursue her bachelor's degree.

She received her Bachelor of Applied Arts and Sciences Degree in Business/Management (1988) and Master of Education in Counseling (1991) Degree from Tarleton State University. She obtained a professional counselor's license from the State of Texas (1993), as well as a professional counselor's supervisor's license. She completed her Doctor of Education Degree in Secondary, Curriculum, and Higher Education from Texas A & M University at Commerce (2006).

She has served Hill College in capacity of vocational counselor (1 yr.), Director of Counseling & Testing (11 yrs.), Dean of Students (1 yr.), Vice President of Student Services (10 yrs.), Director of Behavioral Sciences/psychology instructor (5 yrs.), crisis counselor (5 yrs.), and President (8 yrs.).

She has served as a member of the Texas Association of Community Colleges, vice president and president of the Texas Association of Chief Student Affairs Association and served on several state and legislative committees.

Her accomplishments include securing grant funding to assist first generation college students in making the transition to college from high school, funding for special population students, as well as, acquired federal funding for disadvantaged colleges students. Additional accomplishments include developing the JumpStart Program to provide funding for dual credit students, as well as establishing an early college high school for students attending Burleson and Centennial High School.

Community contributions include serving on the site-based management committee for Whitney High School, Hospice of the Heart Board Member, president-elect of the Hillsboro Business & Professional Women's organization, and the CRCG resource group of Hillsboro. She has conducted numerous professional development workshops for Hill College and the community on topics such as stress management, grant writing, customer service, learning styles, ethics, ADA compliance, wellness, and leadership.

Her teaching accomplishments include the expansion of the Behavior Science Department at Hill College, development of new courses, and integration of virtual technology into the curriculum. She was the recipient of the 2010 NISOD Teaching Excellence award and was nominated by her peers for the Minnie Stevens Piper Teaching award. She was also selected for the Who's Who among American College Teacher's award.

In 2019, she received recognition along with the City of Burleson as a Community College Futures Assembly

Bellwether finalist. She was instrumental in securing Texas Tech University as a higher education partner on her Cleburne Campus and Burleson Center authorizing students to receive a four-year degree, as well as working alongside Burleson ISD and the City of Burleson to develop a new higher education center in Burleson.

In 2008, she published an article in *Community College Times* entitled "Promoting Academic Integrity in Institutions of Higher Education." She has authored monthly articles for the Cleburne Times Review, Burleson Star, and Hillsboro Reporter newspapers.

Accomplishments include being presented as a 2017 Cleburne Rotary Paul Harris Fellow, the Hillsboro 2017 Lions Club Citizen of the Year award, the Hillsboro Chamber of Commerce 2018 Visionary Leader in Education award, inducted in 2019 as the Hubbard Chamber of Commerce Hall of Fame, the 2021 Phi Theta Kappa Honor Society Shirley B. Gordon Award of Distinction, the 2021 Cleburne Chamber of Commerce inductee into the Hall of Fame, and the Cleburne 2022 Good Scout Recipient. Other accomplishments include the 2022 Jessie Jones Leadership award recognized by the North Central Texas Community College Consortium. In 2022, Dr. Boehm was recognized by the Office of the Mayor of Cleburne Texas as Dr. Pam Boehm Day.

Nearing retirement, Dr. Boehm was honored by Hill College by the development of the "Pamela J. Boehm Student Emergency Aid Grant" to assist students to move beyond hurdles they encounter to continue their education.

After a 41-year career in higher education and eight years as President of Hill College, Dr. Boehm spends her time volunteering by interviewing local students for scholarships, enjoying lake life, writing, and hanging out with her family and four grandchildren.